THE
CROOKED PATH
IS PERFECT

FINDING YOUR POWER WITHIN

Satie Narain-Simon, CPA

Defining Moments Press

TESTIMONALS and REVIEWS

"It has been one of my greatest honors to know Satie and to witness the healing power of her story. It brings me great joy and hope knowing that her living beliefs, values, and principles will have a larger space in the ecosystem of our world. She is living proof that no matter where we may find ourselves – life always has a new path to consider".

- **Mpumi Nobiva**, M.A,. Strategic Communications| International Speaker| Artist | Rise Mzansi Provincial Legislature and National Assembly Candidate, South Africa.

"This memoir is riveting. Satie captures the human spirit in its vulnerable state, allowing readers to relate to her experiences in the most profound way".

-**Nathalia Tosta**, MA in English and Educational Administration| High School Teacher, Las Vegas, Nevada

"In her poignant memoir, "The Crooked Path is Perfect", Satie embarks on a courageous journey of self-discovery and self-love that will resonate deeply with readers as both journeys, at their core are, universal to the human experience. Confronting a daunting cancer diagnosis at a pivotal juncture in life, Satie's narrative unfolds with grace and authenticity, revealing her profound transformation through practices like yoga, meditation and alternative healing methods. Her words not only inspire but also serve as a profound guide through adversity, offering solace and

practical wisdom to those seeking resilience and personal growth. Satie's memoir is a testament to the healing power inherent within each of us—a compelling narrative that invites readers to embrace their own journey of self-discovery and empowerment. This book is a stirring reminder that amidst life's trials, we possess the strength to heal ourselves from within through the power of love".

Jessica York, CEO Won Productions |Emmy Nominated Television Host | Producer |Red Carpet Reporter |Dish Network| Chief Badass at Broadcast Like a Badass.

"Satie's memoir beautifully captures the transformative essence of self-love amidst life's trials. Her journey from confronting a cancer diagnosis at a pivotal moment in her life to discovering inner strength through practices like yoga and meditation is profoundly inspiring. Through poignant storytelling and practical insights, Satie illuminates the path to resilience and personal growth. Her words resonate deeply within me, offering solace and guidance to anyone navigating adversity. This memoir is a powerful reminder of the healing power found within oneself—a must-read for those seeking to embrace their own journey of self-discovery and empowerment".

Joseph Lee, Best Selling Author | Founder and CEO JLGOVLLC,| Cyber Board Advisor | Cyber Strategist Consultant | Trusted Advisor

"Satie's memoir is a breathtaking exploration of Love and self-discovery. Her eloquent storytelling not only highlights the transformative power of Love but also reveals how

embodying Love can profoundly impact both our personal lives and society at large. Her journey through struggle to self-realization is both captivating and deeply relatable, offering inspiration and hope to anyone facing challenges. This book is a heartfelt reminder that Love truly is the force that can make our world a better place."

Karim Mirshahi, President Waterfront Media Group| Publisher Waterfront Magazine| Director International Peace Festival

Unlock Your Inner Strength!

Hey there, amazing reader!

We're thrilled to have you embark on this journey of discovering and harnessing your inner strength. To make your experience even more powerful, we've created something special just for you!

🎁 Grab Your FREE Series of 10 Short Videos: "10 Tips to Accessing Strength Within"! 🎁

What's waiting for you?

- Tip #1: Laughter
- Tip #2: Random Act of Kindness
- Tip #3: The Mirror Technique
- Tip #4: The Magic of Gratitude
- Tip #5: Embrace Our Authenticity
- Tip #6: Awareness of the Thought
- Tip #7: Being a Volunteer
- Tip #8: Breath Work
- Tip #9: Connection to Spirit
- Tip #10: Forgiveness

✦ Ready to dive deeper? Here's how to get started: ✦

1. Visit: https://www.youtube.com/playlist?list=PLeaKSOMC0D4vV65SqGvpjOZxsk8zYO3V

2. Enter: Your email address to unlock the videos (when this is set up of course)

3. Enjoy: Your journey to a stronger, more empowered you!

You've already taken the first step by opening this book. Now, let's continue this incredible journey together. See you in the videos!

With strength and positivity,

Satie Narain-Simon

Satie's gift to you: Unlock Inner Strength!

You can get a copy by visiting:
https://www.youtube.com/
playlist?list=PLeaKSOMC0D4vV65SqGvpjOZxsk8zYO3V2

DEDICATION

This book is a tribute to all those who have experienced moments of emptiness, where the absence of love obscured the brilliance of the gems we each carry within. The lack of self-esteem, confidence, and validation often stems from forgetting that we are inherently loved, irrespective of our circumstances. Remember, you are cherished by the Universal Supreme, or by whatever name you ascribe to the greater force.

I extend heartfelt gratitude to my parents, my earthly gods, for their unwavering dedication and unconditional love. To my beautiful mother and my precious father, my hero, my best friend, thank you for always believing in me and supporting the realization of this book. I love you both dearly.

To my brother, Satesh, who has been the guiding light on my journey, inspiring me with his unwavering belief in alternative modes of healing. He introduced me to the realm of Mediumship and the benevolent Entities of Light. His unwavering inspiration for the realms has been a beacon of light in my journey of discovery and growth, ultimately leading me to the path I was destined to walk.

To my husband, Colin, our journey has been anything but ordinary. Your unwavering support and belief in my abilities means the world to me. I love you.

I express my deepest appreciation to the benevolent spirits, the Entities of Light at the Casa Dom Inácio, for their boundless love and guidance throughout this creative process. I love you all.

To my revered Swami Veda Bharati, my esteemed Guru of the Himalayan Yoga and Meditation tradition, my spiritual grandfather who now resides in the ethereal realm. Your influence extends to the fifth generation of our family, a blessing indeed. I am profoundly grateful for the wisdom you imparted and the timeless connection that transcends earthly existence. My heart overflows with love and reverence for you.

To my beloved grandmother, now a celestial presence among the stars, my dear Nanee, whose steadfast faith in a luminous tomorrow remained unwavering. Your boundless love surpasses earthly confines, and my heart is forever filled with love for you.

And to my loyal fur baby, Benji, your constant companionship, unconditional love, wagging tail, affectionate kisses, and soulful gazes have been a source of immense comfort and joy during the many hardships faced during this journey. You have sacrificed your tiny self in so many ways; I will never forget. I cherish and adore you, my little darling, Benji.

Figure 1: With parents at Casa Dom Inacio

Figure 2: Benji

Figure 3: One of my happiest days,
my wedding

ACKNOWLEDGEMENT

To my dad, my hero, and my best friend, thank you for your unwavering support and encouragement throughout this entire journey. From the very beginning to this moment, you have been my confidant, keeping the flame of possibility alive. Despite the challenges and moments of dimmed hope, your constant push and belief in me never wavered. I am forever grateful for your presence and guidance. And to my beautiful mother, whose unwavering conviction always knew that this dream would become a reality, I love you, Mom.

To my sister, thank you for your support throughout my trials and tribulations of writing this book. Your input has been invaluable, and I am deeply grateful.

To Nathalia Tosta, thank you for your invaluable insight and perspective from a different angle during this writing process. Your background in English proved to be a significant asset, offering constructive critiques and feedback. Despite your demanding schedule as a dedicated high school teacher while pursuing your Principal studies, you remained a constant presence, always ready to question, correct, and cheer me on. I am deeply grateful for your unwavering support and friendship.

To Jessica York, my beautiful mentor in the realm of broadcasting, I extend my deepest gratitude for your boundless encouragement in moments of adversity and self-doubt. Your empowering messages served as a guiding light, dispelling the shadows of imposter syndrome. I cherish your gift of friendship and am overjoyed to have your contribution grace a chapter in this book.

To Mpumi Nobiva, you embody the roles of a confidant and mentor and feel like a daughter to me in many ways. Your wisdom surpasses your years, and your presence is a precious gift to me. I am overflowing with gratitude for the privilege to have your contribution grace a chapter in this book. You hold a special place in my heart.

TABLE OF CONTENTS

Preface

I came to a realization: my time on this planet solidified for me that this thing we label as "Love" really is the answer to ALL. My book is a memoir with the message of Love, detailing how my life changed before and after illness. I used my own personal tools to journey within. Why, one might ask? Because of the realization that "Love" really is the answer, and by journeying within, we get to access our superpower: "Loving Self." A term thrown to the wind, a buzzword these days, the truth is that accessing self-love is the driver to gaining strength, courage, confidence, and self-esteem, equaling "Love Within." If I didn't have this foundation, I wouldn't have survived a cancer diagnosis at the happiest time of my life—my wedding.

I've tried for years to block the memory of pain, the pain my heart felt for decades. Have you ever felt side swept, the rug pulled out from under you because of a life event that happened at some point in your life? Only this time it sucked the life out of you—it could be a breakup, illness, loss of work, divorce, or addiction. For me, it was always about affairs of the heart. You see, LOVE was and still is the most important thing for me. Perhaps this notion took root as a youth when I was uprooted because of the political situation from my loving family in Guyana to live in a foreign country, here in Canada with strangers—relatives, but strangers. The journey of "lack" reared its ugly head, for I didn't feel wanted or loved. I felt the presence of something missing in my life; the absence, the sense of an unfulfilled desire to be loved. My heart seemed to always be in turmoil; there is no logic for affairs of the heart, and my heart longed for love. The big one occurred just prior to my huge production of a wedding date—I was dumped! My future was shattered in a blink; broken dreams, shame, and embarrassment started the dive into the depths of darkness and sickening thoughts. One could imagine, after years upon years of this vicious cycle, what the impact could be on wellness on all levels—definitely the cells of the body. And the cells have intelligence, don't they?

Unfortunately, all the prior years of dark thoughts led to cell abuse, and my path took a twisted turn. I was diagnosed with cancer at the happiest time of my life, as a new bride. Through pain, I found my true authentic self! *"The challenge became the transformation"* (*Melanie Warner*).

I was equipped to handle this twist on the crooked path, for I had done the work of journeying within prior, and I felt loved within. I had to have faith, so I followed the turn on my path. This was because I did the work; I applied my personal tools such as:

- Yoga
- Meditation and prayers
- Listening to motivational talks
- Reading books, becoming more aware of my thoughts and what I was allowing to enter
- Mirror talk
- Affirmations
- Gratitude journal
- Visualization

I want my audience to know that their circumstances don't define them. We all have the right to feel loved; it's our birthright, and we were born perfect. Our environment and other external factors can take their toll, so we need strength within. I understand that life can sometimes throw unexpected challenges our way, leading to a sense of unfulfillment. It's not uncommon for folks to experience periods of darkness or uncertainty during these times. To go on this journey, having the courage to fall in love with "I," gives us self-esteem, in turn confidence, leading to the ultimate strength and power within. No one can take this away from us once acclaimed. We don't depend on external factors for validation.

My hope is that through sharing my trials and tribulations with the tools I used to eventually dig myself out of the hole of heartache, I will resonate with many of you. I was able to start to heal from the mental, physical, emotional, and spiritual suffering. In sharing is healing—sharing the lessons I needed to learn, and the truth is I don't want others to go through the pain I went through. I don't want you to go through the number of years I took to get to a place of love within. I want to share the tools I used to get myself out of the quicksand of dark thoughts to loving myself, finding self-esteem, confidence, and strength.

If only I could spend some time with my thirty-year-old self, if I had access to the information and tools, so much heartache would not have happened. There wouldn't have been the fallout of the various levels of life—mind, body, and spirit. I am sure I am speaking to so many of you, am I right? I would have known that, absolutely, we are all beautiful, loved, and cherished by the Creator. My journey to truly loving myself came as a result of many years spent on self-improvement, consistently, day after day; I call it "being in my school of mind training." Then one day, many years later, I found myself really believing that I am truly loved from within; this was the most profound, powerful feeling one could possess. I became so happy, felt so royal, overjoyed at the power of loving myself with all my imperfections. My imperfections became perfect because I truly love myself.

In the following chapters, I am going to share a few life stories occurring after a cancer diagnosis, where walking my crooked path took a 180-degree turn. Meaning that I love myself, but we get shaken up here and there along this journey called "Life." We need to tweak, oil the machine per se, to get back on track, and hence the transformation. The transformation the book offers is that when we truly believe that we're loved by the universal power, and that we are "LOVE," we are connected to the Divine; we then gain our superpower of strength through self-esteem, confidence, and inner validation. Believe me, you too will transform. I am witness and proof of this; I feel the strength within me, and with conviction, I know that I am loved.

Literally, my life changed from the day of surgery onwards. The turn on the path took me to this remote little energetic area off the beaten path of Brazil. My life changed, and I found my spirit connection, a true love. My hope for you, dear reader, is that there is something you will gain; my hope is that the following pages empower YOU to love your imperfect, perfect self.

CHAPTER ONE

How I got Here

For me, I was dabbling in this and that, but it was the cancer diagnosis that kicked me onto a definite path. My brother was the instrument that started the engine and directed the vehicle onto the red brick road (next chapter), to that remote little area off a beaten path in Brazil. Each story shared is a part of my journey, my perception, my reality.

My life changed witnessing a man, his body being used as a host for incorporation by a benevolent spirit, referred to as an Entity of Light. This can be described as observing the presence and influence of a higher spiritual being within the human vessel. It was a powerful transformative experience for me; even now as I write, I cannot believe what my eyes have witnessed. We humans need proof, and I needed proof, which I got when the Medium incorporated with a spirit, an Entity of Light, gave me direction for my life.

I can understand how some would think this is impossible, maybe I have gone "foo foo," but believe me, I am a sane CPA, tax auditor by profession. I've witnessed at this point in time too many events to count. My life changed in a phenomenal manner. How? By actually believing, truly believing that there is a bigger picture, there is more to this life than meets the eye, so to speak. We are loved; we are Love. This is truly an indescribable feeling.

I want you to know that this "love" directs me. I feel like something, someone is guiding me. I can't see it, but I know at this stage in life I am pivoting to something else, and I know and feel that it was all set up this way on purpose by the Divine, the Higher Power.

The end game is through my twisted path, I found true love, and through love, we truly believe we are worthy, we are loved, and we are all made in the same image of the great Creator. Being authentic and true to ourselves really makes us resilient, bulletproof. I believe there is a grassroots movement that each of us matters, our stories matter, we are one collective; this is how we will contribute to making the world a better place.

It sounds so simple, but we get swirled by the waves of culture, environment, religions, politics, and somewhere along the line, we forget who we really are. This included me. Each of us has our own individual journey, experiences, and lessons to learn. I believe we somehow choose our experiences before birth.

Through all of my struggles, mostly emotional, resulted in a reinvention of self. I am so in love with me, my Being. I am comfortable in my skin, true to myself, my authentic self. As my husband would say, "he could not find anyone else that loves oneself more than me and couldn't compete." For me, that is such a compliment because I can rely on my love for me. I am confident about this; this is where I gather my strength.

My hope is that you conclude with this too, and that you too, if needed, find the courage to journey within, accessing your superpower. Why? Self-love is where we gain confidence, self-esteem, and courage. The outer influences make no difference to our cores, so we stay in equilibrium with our stance of self-love, the power within, and that our circumstances don't define us; we are made with the same royal weave of our Universal Father. Why go through so much pain inflicted by our own selves? Just think how much it matters to know that you are loved, you deserve to be loved, and you and I are made in the same image of the almighty Universe!

CHAPTER TWO

This Happened

I remember when my brother, Satesh, brought me here to Abadiania, a place I had never heard of before. *"Where on the map is this place?"* I wondered. *"What is this place?"* Thoughts raced through my mind. I heard him say with conviction in his voice, *"This place is where miracles happen."* Really? I didn't know what to think when he first mentioned this place, let alone 'miracles'. Could it be possible? I felt excitement - Miracles? I mean, I've heard of miracles, but generally, they only happened in the past, in the olden days, when Lord Jesus was alive, or with the Rishis from the East, or the special Natives in the jungle. This couldn't be possible in our normal world, in our current times. Thoughts raced through my mind, yet I felt excited about the possibility. Could it be true, miracles?

Just a few weeks prior, I was experiencing the happiest time of my life. Gee, I was finally getting married. I had been single for so many years, and my biological clock was ticking away. I was so excited, imagining being a mother sometime soon. It was my dream to be a mother, to have a happy family with the white picket fence. I love children; I think it's a miracle, the conception of life. I was getting married to a wonderful man from California, one of my favorite places, and I was planning to live there. So many exciting things were happening for me - planning my wedding, seeing the happy faces of my loved ones celebrating 'Me'. Wow, I was going to be a bride, wonderful! My beautiful wedding dress, the first dress I saw, fit so beautifully. Everything seemed so magical.

It was one week before the wedding, lying on my back on my bed, chatting with a friend from New York about the wedding and her travel plans, when my hand unconsciously touched my breast. I felt a hard lump at the bottom of my left breast! I jumped out of bed and ran to the mirror, lifted my arms, and 'yes', I could see the lump. It wasn't there before; I check every month. I know my body, the lump was not there a month ago, and here it is, at the 6 o'clock position. I felt scared and wondered if I got hit by the kids in Tae Kwon-Do. I was preparing for my Black belt; the kids love kicking, and during our sparring, their legs could reach the bottom of my breast. I felt worried but got back on the phone with my friend, discussing her travel plans to witness my happy day.

That was over nineteen years ago, when my life was turned upside down. Was it fate? My life's plans, dreams, all came crashing down as my life was about to change forever - my body, my thoughts, my husband, our dreams, our lives, expectations, everything thrown out the door. A verdict came crashing down on us, like an avalanche. Here I was in October 2004, a new bride, sitting with my husband, waiting for a day surgery to remove a fibroid in my left breast, when the surgeon walked in. He couldn't look at me, staring straight ahead. Then he said, "*cancer, maybe mastectomy.*" His words faded as I was transported into another world, screaming for my Universal Father! I was given the verdict of a cancer diagnosis, stage two breast cancer, triple negative, with an aggressive rate of growth. Was this karma, as a few have mentioned? What had I done in my previous life? Is it 'sow and so shall we reap'? I had asked my guru, Swami Gi Veda Bharati, whether I was a murderer *or something horrid in a previous life* to experience this fate. He said it was my 'high emotions' personality, and environmental factors. Perhaps he didn't want to hurt my feelings, or perhaps it was an experience for my soul. I lean more towards the idea that I chose this fate or at least the circumstances, even before I was born.

I remember meeting a spiritual authority, Ram Dass's secretary, on my very first trip to Abadiania in 2005. He made quite an impression. Ram Dass, from what I know, was quite up there in the spiritual group in the United States; he lived in California. Anyway, his secretary - I remember our first meeting. Was this by chance or not? I remember seeing him for the first time, the look he had in those penetrating eyes that seemed to draw you in. He looked different, with his hair pulled back into a ponytail, and had an aura around him that attracted one into his presence. His eyes locked into yours; that was what happened with me. It was almost as if his stare was looking into the depth of my soul. I remember asking him, 'why me?' He said that I chose this experience before birth. He said that I was being nudged and didn't budge, then nudged again. I was dislocated from the Source; cancer reconnected me to the Source, and that I hadn't done anything wrong. An interesting thought, isn't it?

I have to be honest, the truth is that it was the day of diagnosis that I also felt the arms of the Universal Father. I remember this so distinctly. As the surgeon couldn't look at me, he was distraught, looking away as he delivered the diagnosis. For the first time, I felt inside me a voice taking over. I heard the silent sound of my voice screaming for my Universal Father, "*It's You and I*". I felt no one else's existence, the conversation between my Father and I reconnected. I had always felt that there was something more for me; I was always somehow attracted to 'spiritual people', other faiths, longing to know more of the other realms, always feeling that we are all connected to the one Spiritual force. At the same instant my conversation started, a nurse appeared out of nowhere, standing in front of me, praying loudly from the Bible. All these events were happening in an open area where others around were witnessing, baffled at what was going on in this corner where my husband and I huddled. Who does that? This is Toronto; it's unheard of. She started praying in her loud, authoritative Caribbean accent, 'With conviction, you are Saved!!' I felt like a child in God's palms. Two other doctors showed up at the same time, looking at me with so much love. They each took a hand of mine and guided me to the surgery room. My journey started; who does this, such love, holding each hand of mine? I don't think this is routine; I know it had to do with my Father. Everyone in the surgery room was kind and compassionate. The surgeon, whom I knew was going to do his best, in his power, to get rid of everything. The nurse showed up again and started praying. I stared into her pupils as I was losing consciousness. I never saw her again; no one had heard of her. I asked and looked for her in vain. Who was she? Why has no one heard of her? In my 'book', she was from the hand of the Universal Father, and certainly an angel!

My brother excitedly mentioned that he found a place that would heal me, no doubt whatsoever. He was 1000% convinced. I did not realize while all the shocked commotion was taking place around me; he was busy researching the entire world for a healer. *'How did people cure themselves 100 years ago?' He asked. 'How do the natives in the jungles heal themselves?'* He did not even want me to do chemotherapy; he was so sure about his comparison. My family and I had never heard those things in 'today's' world. These are things that happened when the world was more pure, I suppose. During this time he was researching, this 'Man' in Brazil kept popping up.

He found other 'special people' around the world; however, there was something about this 'Man' in Brazil that kept my brother's keen interest. He got some information from folks in Australia who had witnessed the Miracle Man's works firsthand. He also got in touch with the author of the "Book of Miracles" and even spoke to a few Broadway dancers about their experiences with the Miracle Man. Then he got in touch with Ricardo, a special guide and owner of a bed and breakfast place, Dom Ingrid, in Abadiania, Goias, Brazil. Ricardo guided him on what and when to take me to this place. He indicated that my brother should take me three weeks after all my treatments were completed. With this information, Satesh was convinced that this was where I needed to be. I remember the hospitals were told about this intention. Princess Margaret Hospital was concerned; however, my oncologist at St. Michael's hospital was curious. I suspected that she did a little 'read'. For ten years, being in her care, she would always be excited to hear the details of my yearly trip. Then she would say, *'whatever you are doing in Brazil, keep doing it; you are doing amazing!'*

My life ended and rebirthed as I traveled to this far, far away land... my faith muscle's roots taken firmly into the ground.

Arrival in Brazil – The Dirt Brick Road

At 10:10 PM on May 29, 2005, my journey began – my brother and I aboard Air Canada, en route to an unknown adventure. Not sure what awaits us, but I feel excited. My life ended and rebirthed as I traveled to this far, far away land...

The first leg of our flight from Toronto to Sao Paulo would take close to 10 hours, the longest flight I had taken so far. When my brother was planning this trip, I thought since Brazil is next to Guyana, our home country, it would only be about a 6-hour flight to our destination, similar timing to Guyana. Imagine my surprise when the flight was close to ten hours; I couldn't believe our neighboring country was so vast. Upon arrival in Sao Paulo, I was in shock – the advancement of this place compared to Guyana amazed me. I used to think only North America was advanced, but my perspective shifted after this adventure; I felt proud to be part of this continent. Sao Paulo, one of the largest cities in the world with over twenty million people, made Guyana, with its fewer than a million people, seem quaint. Sao Paulo looked like a ten times larger Manhattan, while at that time, Guyana had just one high-rise building, the famous Pegasus hotel, near my childhood home. I had never seen a hotel room key control so many things: turning off lights, air conditioning, and television. The people and culture reminded me of Europe – beautiful faces and fit bodies.

The flight to Brasilia from Sao Paulo took about 1.5 hours, confirming that I was truly on a journey with no turning back – nearly twenty-two hours of travel time to my final destination.

Upon arrival in Brasilia, our planned taxi didn't show up, leaving us unsure of what to do in a place where no one had heard of our destination. Not speaking Portuguese added to the nerve-wracking situation, but we eventually found a taxi driver who, although unfamiliar with the area, knew the general direction. The drive to Abadiania, about 1.5 hours from Brasilia, took us from the capital city toward the countryside, offering magnificent views of vast, rolling landscapes. The deep green pastures and trees typical of the Amazon land were breathtaking. The cows, all white, seemed symbolic of the heavenly journey that lay ahead.

As we approached Abadiania on its red brick road, I felt a mix of excitement and nervousness. Driving down the street, we passed "Posadas," or bed and breakfasts in Portuguese, lining both sides. It was a Tuesday afternoon, and foreigners dressed in white looked curiously at our passing car, anticipating who was arriving to start their special journey.

Our Posada, Dom Ingrid, painted in green, orange, and yellow, greeted us with an unexpected charm. I had expected something simpler for a spiritual retreat in terms of accommodation, area, and surroundings. I had imagined that spiritual environments required a minimalist approach, but I was pleasantly surprised; one didn't have to be in rags to be spiritual. Walking into the common area – dining room, TV room, and bedrooms lined up adjacent to each other – I noticed a central courtyard with a large bird cage and lovebirds singing joyfully. The colors and scents of the flowers, the birds, and the red brick road contributed to the South American holistic feeling. Our bedroom, painted in a soothing green color, had clean marbled floors, a simple bed, a place for clothes, and a bathroom. According to my brother's research, this Posada was located within a vortex. I had heard the term before but didn't know much about it at the time. According to Google, vortexes are *"swirling centers of energy conducive to healing, meditation, and self-exploration."* The earth felt alive with energy in this place, something I would experience over the years visiting this special sacred place. I felt like I had been injected with a heavy dose of a love potion.

That evening, as I approached the sky-blue iron gates of the Casa, I sensed a peaceful stillness enveloping me. The flat, soulful blue buildings exuded a quietness where even speaking felt like disturbing the peace. The melodies of tiny yellow songbirds filled the air, their songs blending harmoniously with the natural frequencies of Mother Earth, a revelation I had heard discussed in a podcast.

The "Lookout," a huge platform, offered breathtaking views of the terrain and beautiful sunsets. The sunset over the skyline, with its greenery lining the hilly valley, was spectacular. People sat quietly on benches or stood, taking in the scene, some in meditation, radiating a profound stillness. I met an Australian lady who had brought her brother-in-law, seriously ill, to the Casa. She shared her amazing experiences, describing the Medium as the most powerful healer on Earth. She showed me x-rays and medical tests as proof of the healings she had witnessed. She recounted how her brother-in-law, who should have died from severe spinal injuries in a work accident, had dreamed of coming to Abadiania and miraculously survived a harrowing journey, including a hospitalization in Brasilia. When I first met him, he looked robust, with a radiant glow on his face that seemed almost angelic. *Despite having faced death numerous times, he hugged me warmly, promising to pray for me. Such experiences made me question what was considered possible in 2005; such miracles were usually associated with historical figures like Jesus or prophets, not the present day. Yet, I began to challenge my own definition of normality.*

Dinner offered a variety of choices: salads, rice, chicken, and a variety of vegetables, all delicious. After dinner, everyone gathered to meet Ricardo, the manager of the Posada, translator, and integral figure at the "House of Dom Inacio," translating our questions to Portuguese for the Entities of Light and back to us. Each person could ask three questions, possibly to manage time and the number of people needing attention at the Casa. Ricardo briefed us on what to expect the next day, Wednesday, the first of three weekly sessions at the Casa. I felt neutral, devoid of emotion or expectations, yet nervous and excited. I wondered if I would exude the same humility and bliss as the people I had seen that day. I deliberate and take my time before accepting anything, not easily swayed by words alone; I rely on personal experiences to form my beliefs. This was uncharted territory, a blank slate without preconceived expectations, though a hint of nervous anticipation began to creep in. Tomorrow held the unknown.

I started the next day early, offering prayers and enjoying a delightful breakfast. I admired how Dom Ingrid presented a vibrant array of watermelon, tomatoes, bananas, mangoes, pineapples, along with delightful Portuguese cheese bread and large rolls. Watching Europeans enjoy these treats with butter and jam offered a fascinating contrast to North American breakfast habits.

I also noted their preference for strong black coffee with sugar after lunch, aiding digestion, while in North America, multiple cups of coffee with cream and sugar are the norm in the morning – a habit I must admit being guilty of.

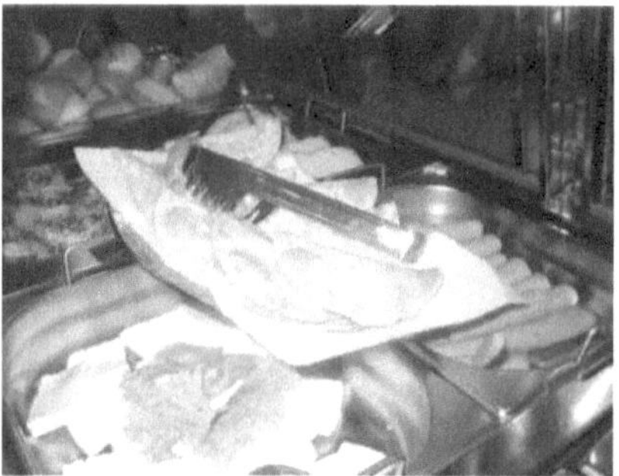

Figure #1 &2 - Morning Delights.

CHAPTER FOUR

Entrance to the Spiritual Place: Casa Dom Inacio

Many have heard of Medium Joao and his healing center, Casa Dom Inacio de Loyola. From what I understand, Medium Joao is probably the most powerful Medium alive at this time and must rank among the greatest mediums. His *"gift"* is not hereditary, nor learned from books. As the author Pellegrino stated in *"Miracle Man"*,

"The Medium, as a teenager traveling the country looking for work, followed a vision of Santa Rita and found himself at the Spiritist Center of Christ the Redeemer. It was there that he had his first experiences as a Medium, performing more than 50 healings in a single day. After an intense period of spiritual instruction and guidance from the spiritual entities that incorporate his body, he dedicated

himself to his healing work discreetly, occasionally suffering persecution and imprisonment for it. These entities are spirits of deceased doctors, surgeons, healers, and theologians who are of such high soul elevation that they no longer need to reincarnate on our physical plane. Using his body as a vessel, these Entities of Light are able to perform miraculous operations and cure the sick."

The Medium was directed to build his Casa in this particular area, a remote little area in the Goias region of Brazil. The area is a spiritual portal that lies within a Vortex, meaning a very high energy field. It is here that the Casa was built, sitting on a plateau of crystal in the ground underneath. According to the author Pellegrino, *"there are main co-ordinate points, sources of energy, like invisible power points. They act as psychic generators, propelling what is not in the physical form."* The Casa is believed to be one of these locations. I heard or read somewhere, maybe in this amazing book about life in the spirit world, "Nosso Lar", actually dictated by a spirit and written by Francisco Candido Xavier. Anyways, it was mentioned that apparently, the spot where the Casa lies is where other planes exist right above, three spiritual planes; the existing one as we know it, one right above, and another above that. Could you imagine this? How far have we come, including myself, to entertain "out of the box" thoughts, letting the mind wander to the vastness of this Universe? It blows my mind to think that it is really limitless. It is sometimes still so difficult to comprehend;

however, what I do know is that going to Abadiania has really expanded my mind beyond my imagination.

Here is a little description of the Casa through my lens, so you can picture it as you come along on this journey with me. The gates, the building blocks of the Casa, are in soulful spiritual colors of blue and white. As you walk through the gates, you start to feel different; at least that is how I feel almost every time I walk through them, like stepping into another time zone. You can hear the birds singing—it's like an Eden's garden in the middle of the grounds, with fruit trees known in the Amazon everywhere. I cannot understand how someone could lack food here, with trees in the wild bearing fruits like guava, five fingers, avocado, cherry (which is called "acerola" in Portuguese and has five times more vitamin C than an orange). The birds—parakeets, parrots, toucans—how I love birds; they feel heavenly, like my spirit animal. I could sit for hours in silence on one of the beautifully carved benches scattered along the landscape overlooking the vast luscious valley, the trees, the magical blue skies, and listening to the birds—ahhh. It is so peaceful, with the little yellow birds singing so beautifully and then there are the ugly, little, cute black ones. Boy, do they have a voice. They are loud, and their tunes are so different from the others; they sing so beautifully. I could hear four to five different tunes at once, all coordinating so beautifully—the rooster gets his turn here and there, the dog digging the ground making that tune to coordinate, maybe a bark here and there, some kind of fly buzzing, crickets, and other sounds I do not know, the cat faintly meows—these are all the sounds of this magical place where the Casa resides.

Then there is the "Outlook", a pergola with wooden benches overlooking the lush valley, the gigantic blue sky, and the path towards the Cachoeira, the sacred waterfall. Here, folks sit in silence in contemplation, meditation, or just as observers.

Everything here somehow looks sharper; the sky I swear has very distinct colors and shapes. I am reminded of a time during my sunrise walk along the prayer trail, a pathway adjacent to the gates of the Casa, where I took a picture of the sky showing a beautiful soft red color with the distinct shape of a hand, palm facing outwards, reminiscent of Michelangelo's depiction of "Heaven creating Man" at the Vatican. I have also observed so much here at night, including witnessing a UFO—I still cannot believe what I saw, capturing Orbs from this "Lookout", energy forms over the Cachoeira (Sacred Waterfall)— unbelievable, the viewings of the night sky from my vantage point.

In the center of this Eden's garden sits a statue of Santa Dom Inacio, with a logo beside it that reads, "Que a Paz prevaleca no Mundo, May Peace Prevail on Earth". Besides the statue, people have adorned it with flowers and crystals—I like to place my crystal there for a moment to be recharged while I say a prayer of gratitude to Santa Dom Inacio. I was not born a Christian, and I do not know much about the different Saints; however, one quickly feels the connection to the one Universal Power. Like my father would say while I was growing up, "All the rivers flow into the same ocean". I truly live this way; this is how I see things, and I surely connect internally to all these beautiful Saints. I am so grateful for all that I have received. Scattered natural quartz crystals around the garden really reinforce the images of the plateau of crystals lying beneath the Casa grounds. Peeking between the trees are the blue and white colors of the area where the crystal bed sessions take place. There are a few rooms where one is directed by the Entities of Light to have these crystal bed sessions.

Now, what are these crystal beds, you may ask? A crystal bed is a bed where crystals are aligned from above in a contraption along the chakras of the body, emitting the attributed colors. They work on one's energy and the seven main chakra energy centers. The healing frequencies cleanse, balance, and open these energy fields. Each color corresponds to a specific energy center associated with a color; your etheric fields are balanced by these spiritual beings. Work is done on the physical, mental, and emotional bodies. I love room #7; it faces the valley, and I would leave the door open so I can hear the birds, the rustling of the trees, and one of the Casa dogs usually would walk in to pay a visit. I have a chapter on the Crystal Bed detailing a few of my experiences.

There is a meeting area with a stage, the walls filled with pictures of the Entities of Light, Deities of many, including Lord Jesus, and orbs scattered across the two side walls and the one facing the audience. In the middle of the stage on the hall hangs a huge wooden triangle. Many have put their heads here with their petitions for loved ones, leaving notes of requests and pictures for healing. So many have put their heads in this triangle with faith and hope for assistance for their loved ones, including our pets, that there is a visual indentation of the Mother Mary imprinted by the masses of heads over the years. This triangle symbolizes faith, charity, and gratitude. Its shape is reminiscent of pyramids, the human body's shape in meditation, and it's also the symbol of "Father, Son, and Holy Ghost". One can easily see that it has meaning to all walks of life. Below the triangle sit two massive pieces of crystals emitting their alluring energies.

Adjacent to the stage is a beautiful soulful blue door that opens up, leading inside the Casa, where most of the work is done by "US" and the Entities of Light. As you enter, this area is called the "First Current". Anyone can sit here; no permission is needed. It is here where the hard work occurs, as Grainee, the dedicated Irish woman who provides English explanations and guidance of the work of the Casa, would say. In this "Current", we freely give our energies to help cleanse the patrons as they walk towards another elongated area called "The Entity Room". In the First Current, great work is being done as some patrons carry dense energies with them. It is like a washing machine; we assist with the cleansing, so by the time the folks are in front of the Entity, a lot of good vibrational energies are already at work. Remember, the word "Entity" refers to the high-level spirit incorporated into the Medium's body. All eyes are closed; this is how the energy works—opening one's eyes breaks the cycle. I heard it even pains the Entity/Entities as they need our energies for them to perform their work. We are like a manufacturing plant generating energies—a current that the Entities of Light need to do their work; they depend on us because we are all connected. We give selflessly here to the work; it's all for others. "Giving is receiving", as Grainee would say.

Right across this area is the "Recovery Room", where folks go after physical interventions if needed. In prior years, we would say "physical surgeries"; nowadays, one has to be careful of the terminology used. The elongated room directly in front of the Entity's chair is called the "Entity Room". The energies from the folks sitting here are used by the Entities of Light for the work being done. Fellow mediums, like myself, do not need permission to sit here; we can sit anywhere. Others have to ask permission or are directed by the Entity to sit in this room. Alongside the front, by the Entity's chair, are other chairs where high mediums sit, or sometimes the Entities ask patrons to sit there, either to use their energies or work on them. I have been asked to sit here a few times by the Entity of Light;

it was quite an experience, I must say. There are other areas, like the right side of the Entity's chair known as the "Entity's Current", where the Entity could send you to sit for a special reason or to continue receiving help from the Entities, among many other reasons. Who knows what the Entities are thinking; all I know is I have been sent there many, many times after seeing the Entity, and it always felt so special. There are many rules, most set by these spirits and some by the assistants of the Casa. I have felt so emotional, experiencing so many feelings—I could go on and on.

On every trip, I would have a meeting with the Medium, bringing him little trinkets from Canada and Las Vegas, and I loved watching his childlike behavior as I explained each item. I would also share photos taken the prior year and pictures of interesting Orbs I captured. Orbs are special energy forms captured on camera. He would then always direct me to go through the back door to that area, the area on the right of his chair known as the "Entity's Current" room to sit. I always felt that it was his way of giving me a gift or showing appreciation. There is one more room at the back where the spiritual surgeries or interventions occur. From this room, there is a door leading to the side of the Casa where the volunteers explain the rules to follow after a spiritual intervention. Rules are important; they provide us with guidance, most of which are from the Entities of Light. I cannot begin to comprehend the Spirit World, but what I do know is that there must be a darn good reason to have these rules. As the priest I met from another South American country said to me, "it is like baking the 'tres meil leiche', a complicated Mexican cake. One has to follow the precise method of instruction to get the result." By the way, this is truly an amazing cake; it really is delicious.

Figure 1- Entrance to Casa Dom Incacio

CHAPTER FIVE

First Experience at the Casa & Entity Incorporation

June 1, 2005 – We arrived at the Casa before 8 AM and headed to the Casa shop to get tickets labeled "1st time (primeira vez)." This indicated that neither our picture or ourselves had previously been in front of the Entity. We then proceeded to the meeting place, where I noticed a café on the grounds before seeing Medium Joao. I was both nervous and elated as I approached him. A wave of emotion flooded through me, and I felt a profound sense of humility. Instinctively, I bowed and touched his feet, a gesture of ultimate respect, before embracing him. Though others stared, they did not approach him. The Medium seemed pleasantly surprised by my display of humility and love.

Reflecting on that first day, I had just completed treatments for breast cancer and was still reeling from the experience. Newly married and unable to relocate to the US, I had heard of miraculous events unfolding in this distant land – you can imagine the mix of emotions I felt.

My brother and I proceeded to the main hall and found seats in front of the stage. Medium Joao emerged and delivered a speech, emphasizing that he does not perform any actions; it is God's work, and continued healing can occur anywhere. The Medium's presence was undeniable. His tall, broad stature exuded strength and authority, while his commanding voice resonated with power. However, it was his eyes that truly captivated – there was something undeniably unusual about them, drawing you in with their enigmatic stare. His hands, almost otherworldly in appearance, were superhuman in size, adorned with unusual freckles. The Medium's demeanor demanded attention, standing out as extraordinary and compelling in every way. He encouraged prayer in one's own religion, asserting that healing occurs through personal faith. He clarified that while donations are not obligatory, any contributions are not for him but for the Casa's affairs and not for healing purposes. Some individuals, unaware that it is the spirits, including our own, that facilitate healing rather than the Medium, have made substantial donations.

Standing close to the stage with my brother, we observed many individuals ready with cameras and video cameras for action. Even after years of visits to the Casa,

I vividly recall how visibly different the Medium's eyes became during incorporations, depending on which spirit was present. I acknowledge this may sound strange to some, but seeing is believing, and I have witnessed this firsthand. His eyes would change immediately upon incorporation, either widening or maintaining a fixed stare with minimal blinking, sometimes intensifying sternly or softening completely.

I consider myself sane; I do not use any form of drugs, nor am I under hypnosis. To confirm my awareness, I could feel and even pinched myself. Yet here I was with my brother in the main hall, surrounded by people dressed in white from various countries, standing or sitting in silence, appearing to be in a meditative state. Moments later, a young foreign girl ascended the platform, barely two feet away from me. A few volunteers stood on the stage, one holding a square silver pan containing a few items and another with a silver bowl of water. Medium Joao took what looked like long scissors from the pan, although they resembled scissors only from my perspective. With one hand, he tilted her head back, holding her steady, while with the other hand, he swiftly inserted the 'scissors' into one nostril, pushing them upward and then pulling them out. In that swift motion, I saw something come out – a lump of some sort. Someone whispered that it was related to her brain. There were no needles visible; this girl was tiny, perhaps size zero or smaller, and she made no sound. I swear to God, this is what I saw. Less than ten drops of blood fell on her white pants and on the floor. How is this possible? The spots of blood were quickly cleaned up, and she was placed in a wheelchair. I saw it happen!! I saw no needles, and she did not utter a sound – I swear to God, this is what I saw. How is it possible that she didn't cry out? She was then taken to the spiritual recovery room. Oh my!! I remain uncertain about the purpose of this specific procedure. Later, I learned that surgeries and eye scraping were common practices, not solely with physical implications but potentially carrying mental or spiritual significance, leaning towards a spiritual interpretation. Subsequently, I discovered that the American girl in question was actually very ill, a fact unbeknownst to me at the time. It's intriguing how individuals may return to their home countries only to find that previously existing physical ailments have vanished or are improving. Some individuals have undergone X-rays and other tests revealing signs of surgery through internal markings. Truly astonishing, a phenomenon unfolding.

My brother and I were dumbfounded and numb, in a state of trance, though he did not faint. He cannot stand the sight of blood, yet here he was in a trance, just staring. I get the tiniest cut and it bleeds like crazy, yet here I was, watching something long being inserted into someone's nose, without anesthesia, with just a few drops of blood falling on her pants and the floor. What was more shocking was witnessing this and hearing no screaming, fear, or pain from the girl. How is this humanly possible?

It makes no sense whatsoever. I have never heard or seen anything like this in people, books, or movies. What was strange is that it all seemed normal to me. My God, I still cannot believe what my eyes witnessed on that first day at Casa, now almost twenty years ago.

I proceeded to the first-time line to meet with the Medium in Entity. As I made my way to the line, unsure of what I was feeling, just observing but becoming very nervous. As I entered the 'First Current' – where people are praying and meditating, their energies are being used to assist the Entities in their work – I was told it is like going through a 'washing machine.' As we pass through, all sorts of energies, both positive and negative, are directed toward us. These people are praying for us, spiritually cleansing us as we move along the line toward the Medium in Entity. Eyes must remain closed at all times for the energy flow to work efficiently. If someone opens their eyes, the energy field stops there. Our eyes also bear the imprint of everything we have witnessed and can pick up negative energies. The people looked serene in their slight variations of white clothing, all with closed eyes. Some had smiles, including the lovely Irish volunteer, Grainne, who read verses from the Bible in English and Portuguese, offering encouraging words to everyone for their good work in contributing their energies. I felt emotional seeing people pray for us silently as we walked through, asking for nothing in return.

Approaching the Entity room, an oblong-shaped space filled with people praying with closed eyes, I could hear the distinct voice of the Entity, unlike any other. There is something about the Entity's voice that commands attention and draws listeners in. The stern tone carried strength and authority. I trembled as I neared the front of the line, facing the incorporated Entity of Light. Ricardo was there, also serving as the Casa's translator, and fortunately, I had stayed at his family's posada. He began recounting to the Entity what had happened to me: my desire to be healed from breast cancer and to have a baby, a long-held dream of mine. I remembered feeling pressured to marry before my biological clock stopped ticking. It didn't go as planned; I had a brief window after marriage but was "stopped in my tracks" by the cancer diagnosis.

Now it was my turn, trembling uncontrollably. I took off my slippers and knelt in front of the Entity, placing my right hand on his knee. Thoughts raced through my mind, *"Wow, this is a spirit in Medium Joao's body."* I looked directly into his eyes; he didn't even let Ricardo finish explaining why I was there. Instead, he scribbled something in an unknown code on a piece of paper. He said *'two crystal baths and surgery'* in the afternoon. I later learned that within four seconds, the Entity sees your blueprint psychically. I still don't know exactly what I felt; I know I was nervous and scared about the surgery. Not a fan of pain, a 'chicken,' I was deeply concerned about the "surgery," but everyone advised me to have faith. There was a choice between physical and spiritual surgeries. "Faith" is often tested, but it's definitely building my faith muscle to another level.

"What is this crystal bath, is it a tub with cold water and crystals?" My thoughts and imagination were running wild. I was scared of the unknown. Later, I found out that it is a room that smelled like sandalwood, with a bed similar to a massage bed, and seven crystals hanging above aligned with the colors of the appropriate chakras. Looking back, I realize I was overcome with fear, not allowing myself to 'open up, let go, and embrace.' I was resistant to the unknown, though subconsciously open while consciously closed.

That afternoon, I nervously went to the "surgery room." In those days, the term used was physical and spiritual surgeries, now known as 'intervention.' Those undergoing surgery proceeded into the same room, where a volunteer prayed in Portuguese. We were asked to close our eyes and not cross our hands or feet, as this would interfere with the energy flow and the work of the Entities of Light. Blocking the energy flow needed by the Entities of Light. We were asked who wanted visible (physical surgery) or intervention, the new term used in current times. I made sure my hands did not flicker. For invisible surgery, we were instructed to place our hands where we desired healing or on our hearts, indicating to the Entities to work on whichever part of the body needed healing. I tried to locate my heart, but couldn't find it. "*Where is my heart?*" I kept asking myself. "*Is it in the middle, by my breast, on my left, or right? Gosh, I do not know, what has overcome me?*" I had this anxious internal dialogue, then heard a distinct, authoritative voice. My eyes shut tightly, scared and having faint thoughts. I could feel my face and the muscles in it, so numb I couldn't feel anything. After a while, we were told to open our eyes and leave the room with our guide, who would explain the rules; "*Stay in our rooms and rest, no sex for forty days or an increase in sexual energy, no pork, pepper, or alcohol for fifty-five days.*" On the seventh night, we were told to sleep in white, put a cup of holy water by the bed, the Entities would visit between midnight to five am, and in the morning to drink the holy water. I was told to stay in my room for twenty-four hours, returning to the Casa to the 'Current' room, and in the afternoon for meditation, prayers, and contemplation.

I wrote my name, date of birth, and location on a piece of paper, dropped it into a box for the Entities of Light to visit on the seventh night. I collected my herbs (pasiflora) from the little pharmacy. Everyone received the same herbs; however, the effect varied among individuals. This depended on what needed to be addressed, whether it be mental, physical, emotional, or always, spiritual.

I returned to my Posada and stayed in my room. I didn't feel well. "*What is going on?*" I kept thinking. "*What is happening here? I saw nothing, felt nothing, yet here I am, feeling unwell for no apparent reason.*" I felt fine before going to the Casa. *"Maybe it's a cold I could catch on the long flight. Or could it be these invisible energies?"* Later at dinner, someone told me it was a reaction from my surgery. I also felt hot and then freezing. I didn't want to stay in my room; I wanted to go outside and sit on the bench. We were told to stay in our rooms for this time of reflection, to pray and meditate. We were also psychically open and vulnerable, not wanting to attract negative energies to our open psyches. I couldn't make sense of it all, and I wasn't used to 'staying put.' *"It's not far to walk outside; it's literally just outside my room, and I'm going to go."* Suddenly, I felt feverish! It was as if my mind was being read; I've learned over the years to be aware of your thoughts. The funny thing is, I don't get fevers, never with a cold, but here I was, so cold that my brother had to put two blankets over me. I was shivering and came to the conclusion that it was indeed from the surgery. It was amazing because I am not easily convinced of things, and here I was, having a fever for no reason. I had to give in; it had to be from the invisible surgery. It didn't make sense, but I had no physical exertion, and here I was feeling sleepy and so tired. I know my body, and this was not normal, making for quite an experience for me.

I felt tired and stayed in my room all the next day. The quietness was serene, with only the sound of singing birds. There was no television, no music, and no interaction, yet strangely, I didn't mind. What a contrast from city life in Toronto. That night, I felt energy zaps at the bottom of my right breast. It felt similar to what I experienced when Swami-Gi, my yoga and meditation Guru, initiated me last August into the 'Himalayan Yoga and Meditation' tradition. I felt a strong energy on my left breast, the location of the lump. I wanted the initiation to stop; the energy zaps felt like buzzing, very painful. I sensed something profound unfolding in my life. Little did I know what was yet to come that October!

Now, I believed the Entities were doing work on my breast. I felt the zaps there and, on my uterus, along with a dull pain on the lower left side of my tummy.

Twenty-four hours after my spiritual surgery, I was allowed to go to the Casa for prayers and meditation. I am well-versed in meditation due to my upbringing with parents who are lifelong students, but being here was a unique experience of dedication to silence. Hundreds lined up before eight am to enter the "First Current" for prayers, meditation, and contemplation. The environment was profound, prompting deep thoughts about our purpose, self-forgiveness, and receiving energy from the Entities of Light who also worked on us.

Sitting in one of these "Currents," various thoughts and inner dialogues surfaced – reflections on life events, questions, resolutions, all happening at once. Sometimes, I felt like an observer of these thoughts, like watching a movie play out in my head. These thoughts seemed to stem from a distant corner of my mind, haunting me with unresolved emotions from a past relationship. I found myself trapped in a cycle of heartache and regret, consumed by lingering hurt from a love lost just months before the wedding. Overwhelmed by intense emotions, I neglected my own well-being, unaware of how to break free from negativity. Despite advice to prioritize self-care, I struggled to release the pain that held me captive. I was repeatedly told to take care of myself, noting a common theme among people with breast cancer – they often prioritize others over themselves. It wasn't until I sat in the profound energy of the First Current, feeling the raw intensity of my emotions, that I realized the importance of addressing and processing these unresolved feelings as a crucial step towards healing and growth.

I could hear sounds from the adjacent room, "The Entity Room" – a hissing sound, eerie yet not frightening, as the Mediums balanced energy. I became frustrated – "Why can't I just embrace this?" Looking at others, seemingly sane and intelligent, with unwavering faith, I wondered about myself. Their backgrounds were mind-boggling, yet here they were, believing in benevolent spirits reaching out from another realm. It all seemed surreal to me; I'm not easily convinced. I needed my own process and individual experience before accepting such beliefs. I started to develop a headache, unable to concentrate, and then I felt a prickling sensation in my breasts. Suddenly, I saw a white light flash across my closed eyes three times. *"What's happening? Where did this come from? My eyes are closed; how can I see lights?"* These thoughts raced through my mind in the enclosed building with a roof that had a window. I knew what I saw and felt, yet skepticism crept in. When I mentioned it, others were unfazed, saying, *"Oh, that's normal. We've felt it too; it's the Entities."*

During my stay at Posada, I had the pleasure of meeting a group of young female doctors who shared with me their observations about the increasing number of doctors from the United States, particularly California, visiting Casa Dom Inacio. I was taken aback by the interest shown by North American doctors, as I had previously perceived them to have a narrower focus on pharmaceutical-based healing methods. While the presence of European doctors did not surprise me, the enthusiasm of their North American counterparts was indeed unexpected. These doctors expressed a genuine desire to expand their knowledge and incorporate new healing approaches into their medical practices in Florida. And also they were here on their own journeys receiving some form of healing modality for themselves. It's inspiring to see healthcare professionals seeking to broaden their horizons and explore alternative healing modalities. I concluded that the prickling effects on my breast were from the workings of the Entities of Light; I could feel healing energies where needed through divine intervention.

The morning meditation lasted about two and three-quarter hours. We drank holy water given to us in little plastic cups as we concluded the morning session, then proceeded for the holy soup. The soup, made the same way daily with vegetables, pasta, and a piece of bread, was consistently tasty. Even after two decades of visiting, nothing had changed about the soup—same quantity, same ingredients, same smiles from the serving volunteers. The soup is said to be grounding, and it's a ritual after the morning session to partake in it.

In the afternoon, from 1:45 pm to 4:30 pm, I returned for more prayers, meditation, and energy work. I was supposed to be in the Medium Room, needing permission to sit there. During this session, I felt something profound happening to me. Despite any lingering guilt, I was overcome with intense emotions. I delve further into this experience in another chapter.

My brother underwent a visible surgery today. Unfortunately, I missed witnessing it as I was in the 'Medium Room Current' at the time, unable to find anyone who could provide details. My brother, who typically cannot stand the sight of blood, had unwavering faith and desired a physical surgery. However, the Entities read his thoughts, and he did not receive the physical intervention he expected. According to him, "*I felt Medium Joao put both his hands over my face. I instantly felt transported, like 'beam me up, Scottie' from Star Trek. It was as if I had been beamed to another place.*" He continued, "*I felt the hands over my face, and the surgery was over. Next thing I knew, I was being wheeled into the recovery room. Before that, I touched Medium Joao's feet as a symbol of ultimate respect.*" I regret not witnessing this moment firsthand, yet I trust there is purpose in every experience here, where we become transparent to the Entities of Light.

This chapter vividly illustrates the practical application of strengthening one's faith. Prior to arriving at Casa Dom Inacio, I had diligently exercised my faith through practices such as yoga, prayer, meditation, seeking guidance from my Guru, and drawing inspiration from my father. However, the extraordinary events recounted here propelled my faith to new heights. Witnessing unseen spirits and experiencing phenomena firsthand in this lifetime left me in awe. I still cannot believe what my eyes have witnessed. I found myself stretching beyond my perceived limits to place an unprecedented level of trust, ultimately leading to a profound enhancement of my faith.

In life, we all like to believe that we have faith. We trust in ourselves, in our abilities, and in the path that we've chosen. But let's be honest—there are times when we all struggle with fears. Fear of failure, fear of cancer recurrence, fear of the unknown—these are all common fears that can shake our faith to its core.

CHAPTER SIX

Struggles With Fear

"Fear—if you agree, then it's your agreement that makes it come to pass. Guard your Mind!" Joel Osteen. This is so personal; I am guilty of this, spending years forgiving myself for falling into this trap.

Fear and worry have been my biggest adversaries for so many years, and they still challenge me at times. It's a work in progress, constantly making the decision to dispel thoughts of fear. Fear! Fear! Fear! Fear that I disappointed my family by not working hard enough to pursue a career in medicine. Fear of not being good enough while living with relatives due to the political situation in Guyana, prompted my parents to send me to Canada for a better life. It's interesting how our minds work at a younger age, the thoughts that consume us. Then I graduated to fear of not being smart enough at university, followed by fear that guys were only attracted to me superficially and not for long-term relationships. During the seventies and early eighties, an era fraught with racial tensions towards people of color, which I identified as, it was a tough time for a youth. Coming from Guyana where six races generally lived in harmony, I was never exposed to such skin color prejudice, which certainly contributed to feelings of 'lack'. Self-esteem issues and lack of confidence plagued me, always feeling the need to be more than I was. I feared disapproval from anyone and always felt disapproved of. I suppose many of us go through these feelings when we look back now, don't we? Perhaps it's a part of life, part of growing up, and certainly influenced by our environments.

Fear manifested at various points in my life, and looking back, my fears often became realities. During my marriageable and childbearing years, I feared it couldn't happen to me—marrying my "prince," having a baby, and a home with a white picket fence. I'm not sure why I placed such emphasis on this, but it became increasingly distant. This fear came true when my planned marriage, with all its hopes and dreams for the future, fell apart shortly before the grand event. I firmly believe this dark period contributed to my later downfall. Cells are intelligent; they absorb negativity and remember trauma. I subjected them to a whirlwind of toxicity. I believe all these toxic thoughts were stored in a dark place within me, waiting to strike and leave their mark. After years of this darkness, my resilient body could take no more and finally succumbed. Looking back, it was fear that brought on the illness. I allowed myself, my soul, to suffer. I chose the pain and embraced feelings of unworthiness. I genuinely believe in Darwin's theory, *"survival of the fittest."* Emotionally weakened, I strayed from my source, my true love. I believe in the power of thoughts, but at that time, I was so immersed in sorrow and hurt that I felt trapped, unable to navigate my emotions. I was drowning in misery and couldn't find a way to breathe. Why was I so foolish? Why did this happen? I realized it was because I didn't love myself unconditionally.

I now understand, diagnosed years later with a life-threatening illness, the impact of dark, toxic thoughts. I contributed to my illness. Many of us have been through similar challenges. Abnormal fear—this consumed me. I was terrified of cancer, constantly checking my body for lumps, especially my breasts, almost obsessively. Where does this fear originate? I often pondered. They say fear is man's greatest enemy, and I believe it now. The fear in my mind was real, even though it didn't exist in physical form. I've listened to numerous speakers, read countless articles on this topic, but for me, it was deeply personal. "The subconscious mind takes the fear at your request" (Joseph Murphy). Fear knocked persistently on the door of my mind until it became a reality.

Maybe our fear stems from our deep-seated fear of death. If we truly believe in a higher power and reincarnation—an increasingly common belief—why should we fear death? If death is just the transition from this body to a realm of intense love and happiness, why do we remain so afraid, including myself? I fear leaving this life, my family, and loved ones. I fear the unknown, leaving behind the familiarity I've cultivated in this life. If I truly have one hundred percent faith in a higher power and in the soul's journey through human experience, why do these thoughts still plague me? Deep down, I do have faith in a higher power—I've witnessed miracles in my life and my family's lives. Yet, I question whether my belief is genuine or just lip service. This internal struggle reflects my ongoing journey—a work in progress. I believe we must guard our minds as guardians, nurturing our thoughts with care.

Embrace the profound significance of cultivating self-love, for within lies our superpower—the very essence where we connect with the Divine, tapping into our inherent right to be loved. This internal sanctuary not only fosters self-esteem and confidence but also liberates us from the shackles of seeking external validation. As someone who once navigated life with intense emotions, I've successfully forged a path to self-love by diligently employing transformative tools. Now, I am thrilled to share these invaluable insights with you, my cherished readers, so you can expedite your journey and avoid the years of trial and error that marked my own pursuit of fulfillment. Remember, the tools I used may not perfectly fit your journey, but the essence lies in discovering what resonates with you. Despite the diversity in approaches, the ultimate goal remains the same.

Tools I Use to this Day:

Building the faith muscle through persistence with repetition, as Tony Robbins would say, "repetition is the mother of skill." This is what I did, even when I didn't feel like it.

1. **Creating a Sacred Space:** Immersing myself in what I consider a sacred space has been an essential practice for me—a haven where I feel a deep sense of connection. In my case, this sacred spot resides in a corner of my room adorned with my altar, crystals, incense, and images of revered figures such as Lord Jesus, Lord Krishna, Buddha, and Santa Dom Inacio. This intimate space serves as a sanctuary for stillness and introspection. My devotion unfolds through prayer, guided by a personal mantra bestowed upon me by my spiritual mentor, Swami Veda Bharati. Whether using a rosary or my crystal mala, I engage in the repetition of my mantra, or sometimes simply affirming "I AM," fostering a profound connection. Spending moments in silence, I meditate, transitioning into prayer, extending my intentions to others, and expressing gratitude for the abundant blessings in my life.

Create a personal sanctuary, whether it's your garden or a corner in your home. This special space should evoke a sense of calling and resonate with positive energy. Alternatively, find connection and inspiration in places of worship, relishing the unique atmosphere when surrounded by fellow worshippers. I like to venture to diverse places and experience various sites, adding to the profound feeling of unity, as individuals from different backgrounds converge with one common goal - connecting to a Supreme force.

Remember that repetition is the mother of mastery (Tony Robbins). Even if you don't feel like spending time within, even if you are busy, need to get to work early on a cold, dark winter morning—I understand, but you still have to do it. Once you take action, you'll regret having doubted the practice in the first place. As days pass, this becomes a habit, and that's where we want to be. Voila!

2. **Physicality – Tae Kwon-Do, Yoga, or Gym:** Before cancer, I spent years in my self-created school called "The Mind Training School." Engaging in physical activity was crucial—not just for health but because sweating ignites the happy drug, adrenaline. When I started Tae Kwon-Do, it became a tool that ignited the start of my journey to self-love. I volunteered at the club, from bookkeeping to cleaning toilets to sparring with kids. Despite getting beaten up countless times (kids love to spar!), the sweating and the inner voice urging expression—it was unmatched. The sweat, the pain, the technique that allowed me to break wood—these ignited something within me. It was a tool for building confidence and self-esteem. I worked out several hours a week, a significant shift for someone who

couldn't do a sit-up before Tae Kwon-Do. A mindset shift was underway; I was determined to reach a place of self-love. I'll forever be grateful to Tae Kwon-Do; it changed my life and remains a wonderful tool. I was preparing for my black belt when I received my cancer diagnosis. However, the tools I had honed over years on my personal journey prepared me to endure what was to come.

3. **Yoga Practice:** After cancer treatments, I started practicing yoga. This physical practice worked and still works for me. Yoga unites mind, body, and spirit. Remember, what works for me may not necessarily work for you. The important takeaway is to find something you love that puts you in the frame of mind to go within, to have your conversations with God. Remember, persistence with consistency will do the trick. Once it becomes a habit, voila! You have a tool for life.

4. **The Power of Thought:** It took me nearly a decade on my path to learn to love myself from within. One of the tools I still use to this day is being conscious of the thoughts running through my mind. I am intentional about being aware of arising thoughts and how they make me feel. Are they beneficial for my well-being? I am conscious of what I watch on television, the movies I choose, what I read, who my friends are, and what my family says. I am mindful of what I am feeding my psyche, the thoughts going back and forth. Experts say we have about seventy

thousand thoughts per day, with many being negative. Imagine seventy thousand thoughts—wow! I strive to be aware of my thoughts. When a negative thought pops into my head—and believe me, some strange ones do—I immediately switch the mental image, akin to changing the TV channel. This is a deliberate action. Over time, it becomes easier to do.

Examples of Fear and How I Used My Tools to Calm My Spirit:

1. <u>Early Thursday Morning Trance:</u>
One early Thursday morning, I found myself in a trance-like state, sensing an ominous presence all around me. I felt a pulling sensation in my arms and legs, which felt heavy and real. Despite feeling scared, I began chanting "OM" and the Gayatri Mantra—a prayer to the Supreme in the form of the Sun, which stimulates and empowers the mind. This prayer was ingrained in me since childhood alongside "Our Father who art in Heaven." As I continued, my jaw muscles weakened, and I wondered why the evil atmosphere persisted despite my prayers. Just before 5 am, I heard an unusual sound, and suddenly, the negative vibe disappeared. It dawned on me that spiritual awareness was unfolding—a battle between good and evil where God always prevails. The incident felt intensely real, but the key takeaway was my lack of fear. In the past, I would have been terrified, but now I ride through such

experiences with confidence, trusting in the power of higher consciousness.

2. June 22, 2015 Dream:

On June 22, 2015, I experienced a setback with fear. I had a dream where my oncologist mentioned cancer recurrence over the phone, and I saw a cancerous spot on my leg. Concurrently, I invoked the Entities of Light—spiritual beings I believe can intervene positively in our world. As I focused on them, the lump dissolved, leaving only a faint scar on my leg. It felt tangible, as if the Entities of Light were indeed present. Calling upon these benevolent spirits is a practice I cherish, especially during times of stress or negativity. I've learned to consciously choose positivity and trust in the power of my thoughts, a practice I reinforce daily.

3. Trip in 2016 and Facing Fear:

During my trip in 2016, my struggles with fear surfaced prominently. On my first night at this sacred place after many years, I couldn't sleep. The next day, during the 'First Current' session, fear gripped me intensely. With my eyes closed as part of the session, I felt pressure in my heart area and almost raised my hands for help, overwhelmed with fear. In moments like these, participants are encouraged to trust in the Entities of Light. Desperate, I mentally appealed to them for control over my anxieties and a sense of calm assurance. Suddenly, I felt a surge of energy in my ear drums, heat on my lower right breast, and across my face. I even drifted off to sleep briefly, which rarely happens during the day for me. This indicated significant work by the Entities of Light, as such moments are believed to be particularly beneficial. Despite my closed eyes, I vividly saw birds flying, possibly black birds, a vision that brought clarity. By the end of the session, I felt lightened, as though a heavy burden had been lifted. My breathing became easy and effortless.

Through these experiences, I discovered how to transform fear into fuel, using it to propel myself forward rather than allowing it to hold me back. I share these experiences with the hope of inspiring others facing their own fears. Remember, no matter the fears you confront, faith is like a muscle—it grows stronger with use.

CHAPTER SEVEN

Why Struggling Thoughts?

"What a superb topic today from Joel Osteen (April 6, 2014) - Mindfulness of our thoughts! Thoughts are powerful; they set off motion. 'We will eat the fruits of our words. Poor mouth, poor life.' 'Choose thoughts carefully, thoughts are things,' Wayne Dyer. It's easy to say, but in reality, I found this to be a struggle. It was my fault for allowing myself to be consumed by negative emotions for so many years. Numerous youthful years were spent tormented by negative thoughts. The loss of a relationship left me feeling desperate, useless, unwanted, unloved, and lifeless. Everything seemed to go wrong—'when it rains, it pours.' I lost my job to the early nineties recession, the man I thought I couldn't live without, and failed an exam after eight years of hard work. I felt worthless and dumb for several years.

The cascade of events began with the emotional blow of losing the man I was set to marry in July of 1992. Everything was arranged—the date was fixed, wedding preparations were underway, overseas guests had finalized their travel plans, and even the priest had journeyed from Guyana to officiate our union. However, our dreams of a blissful future came crashing down abruptly. The ensuing feelings of embarrassment, sorrow, and shame not only affected me deeply but also cast a shadow of emotional devastation over my family. Plunged into a state of despair, I grappled with a sense of unworthiness that seemed to define my very being. In reality, it was my own perception of weakness that clouded my self-image at that challenging time. I believe many of you may have experienced moments of self-doubt and unworthiness in your own journeys. It's important to acknowledge and reflect on these difficult experiences.

In the nineties, during that challenging period, I felt as if I were trapped in quicksand, relentlessly sinking without respite. It seemed impossible to catch my breath, and the weight of the situation was overwhelming. Back then, I had no awareness of any self-help tools, and the absence of social media connections meant there was no avenue for sharing personal details. It was a time when reaching out for support and finding resources felt like navigating uncharted waters.

Then, suddenly one day after several years of feeling miserable, I made the decision once and for all to 'Stop!'

and start taking charge of my heart. I committed to change, to feeling better.

This was the start of something exquisite—a moment when the radiant light within me began to emerge.

I used the tools in this book slowly but surely, repeating the same practices day in and day out, until one day I started to feel a shift—I began to feel love unfolding within me.

I've categorized the following tools into "Before" and "After" illness. Before illness, I took a leap of faith and delved into finding my inner strength, cultivating what I call my superpowers to prepare myself for coping with a cancer diagnosis.

Before illness, these were the tools I used:

Spiritual: I've always been drawn to spirituality in various forms—the Universal Power, the Divine. I found solace in visiting places of prayer and connecting with others, united in the goal of connecting to the Oneness. Yoga and meditation have been integral to my journey.

- I practice Hatha Yoga, which focuses on the science of breath. Introduced to my family and my home country of Guyana generations ago by Swami Veda Bharati, a special bond formed between us when I met him as an adult in Toronto. I felt overwhelming love in his presence, earning me the nickname of his spiritual granddaughter.

- Focusing on breath was transformative for me. It helped combat anxieties that had developed over the years. Shifting from chest breathing to diaphragmatic breathing through Hatha Yoga was a game-changer.

Prayers, yoga, and meditation—these three practices intertwine seamlessly for me. While they may not be the same for everyone, they should resonate deeply, stirring the heartstrings and nurturing a love within that words cannot fully explain. Spirituality can manifest through chanting, contemplative walks, or listening to the waves on a shore—anything that connects you to the Silence within. I personally find great satisfaction in praying aloud and feeling a sense of being heard by the Universe. I firmly believe that the Universe listens—a belief you can test through small experiments to experience its workings.

Through consistent use of these tools, day in and day out, I began to feel inner strength, self-esteem, and confidence. My light started to shine, and I felt appreciated from within as the love within me grew.

I continue to use these tools to this day because, as we all know, life throws us curveballs, and we need to return to our toolbox to navigate challenges.

After illness, the Spiritual aspect became more focused. I had to revisit my toolbox and rebuild my "Faith and Belief" muscle.

I discovered another tool that became essential—Casa Dom Inacio, my spiritual home. Known for its inexplicable phenomena, including a vortex with an underground crystal linked to three other planes directly above the Casa, it serves as a conduit for spirits to aid on this plane through human vessels. The Entities of Light, as they're known, perform life-altering miracles that defy conventional belief but are undeniably real. For over two decades, I've frequented the Casa, where I normalized the extraordinary activities and phenomena around me during the initial years. However, returning to Canada, my beliefs often faced challenges and began to waver.

Let me share a few stories illustrating how the Casa and the Entities of Light became a profound tool in renewing and strengthening my faith.

1. During a trip in August 2007, as I knelt in front of the Entity, I gazed into the huge, gentle eyes of the Spirit incorporated in the Medium's body. I asked for my faith to be renewed and sought help for my physical health and to release fears. The Entity assured me of assistance and directed me to enter the "Current," an area on the right side where specific work by these benevolent Entities of Light occurs. Describing the feeling of love that envelops one in these moments is nearly impossible; those who have been there could relate to the overwhelming sensation. As I sat with my eyes closed in the Current, I recalled previous gifts from the Entities, like the time they unknowingly worked on fibroids during my second trip to Abadiânia in June 2006. Before my journey, my doctor predicted I would enter menopause due to chemotherapy treatments.

Defying medical expectations, my regular cycle returned after spiritual intervention, though I later required a DNC to manage excessive bleeding upon returning to Canada. Similarly, despite being informed that my arm would lose sensation after lymph node removal, it regained 99% of its feeling. These experiences renewed my faith in the power of the Entities of Light.

2. On the same trip in August 2007, I encountered another profound experience confronting my "struggling thoughts." One night, feeling uneasy, I slept on my left side and awoke around 1 am with a sensation of paralysis. The following day, during a session with a psychic massage therapist, I speculated about potential spiritual surgery, later confirmed by the therapist. Advised not to exert myself after surgery, I reflected on a recent trip to Brasília. Returning to my lodge, I felt sacred again, experiencing sudden rib pain on my left side—an aftermath of the spiritual intervention addressing my fears.

3. Events continued unfolding during this 2007 trip, including witnessing extraordinary orbs, notably a golden-yellow oblong orb the night before the August full moon. These signs from the Universe reassured me of being cared for and urged me to "keep faith, stay strong"—a reminder of a new normal beyond my previous struggles.

4. The incident that solidified my faith occurred when I decided to wait for the 2nd time line for another opportunity in front of the Entity. Seated beside the stage, I sensed an impending event, despite legal constraints preventing visible surgeries. Medium João faced persistent legal persecution, even as those same legal officials sought healing for themselves or loved ones. The anticipation in the crowd was palpable as the Medium incorporated the Entity, guiding a red-haired British woman onto the stage. The solemn atmosphere intensified as the Entity performed a physical intervention, making eye contact with each of us seated on the side bench beside the stage, affirming a deeper purpose for our shared experience. As he exposed her lower tummy, he kept looking in our direction, I instantaneously knew why. His glance was directed to me, I stood up shaking, tears flowing, I knew why. I felt the language of telepathy for the first time communicating to me. '*I know I do not need any proof, please forgive me. I believe, I will never doubt again*' I said. The Entity then took the knife and made an incision into her tummy. While he was doing this he was looking in our direction again, stuck his finger inside, made a few movements then stitched her up. No matter how many physical interventions I have seen to date, it never ceases to amaze me how one could be looking elsewhere while using a knife to cut, scrape or stitch, just humanly impossible! Overcome with emotion, I captured the moment with my camera discreetly, feeling a mix of fear and awe at witnessing such a sacred event.

The surgical procedure defied logic as the Entity operated swiftly and without visible pain or bloodshed, leaving only a few drops on the woman's pants. This transformative event left us all profoundly moved, bonded by a collective spiritual journey.

The purpose of my trip to Casa Dom Inacio was to confront and manage the turmoil within my thoughts. The experience was profoundly enriching, reaffirming my faith through countless moments of telepathic communication and the reading of my thoughts. I was even invited to sit in a special chair, typically reserved for mediums or those in need of significant spiritual or physical work. Throughout the trip, synchronicities abounded, and I witnessed orbs multiple times. These orbs, spiritual beings, carry healing properties and messages that resonate with both the photographer and the subjects captured.

The energy I encountered was so intense that it overwhelmed me at times. My heart felt ready to burst, I trembled uncontrollably, and I often felt faint. I experienced a burning sensation in my stomach and heard my heart pounding loudly. These physical reactions were unfamiliar until I realized they were responses to my conscious request to feel the Entities of Light. Their energies are profoundly potent, sometimes challenging for our physical bodies to assimilate.

As an ordinary person, I witnessed extraordinary phenomena. These experiences deepened my faith and helped me address the inner turmoil I carried. I used these encounters as tools to navigate and transcend internal conflicts. They were not mere moments but transformative milestones in my journey of self-discovery and spiritual growth.

CHAPTER EIGHT

Gifts Received – Seeing Light, Vibrational Energy

Since my journey to Casa Dom Inacio, I've been blessed with numerous gifts from the benevolent Entities of Light. One of the most remarkable among these is the ability to "see light," which first manifested in 2007. Yes, I said "seeing light." This extraordinary phenomenon occurs during the early hours of my deep slumber, becoming almost nightly occurrences. The sensation of basking in the radiant glow of the sun, feeling its comforting warmth on my face, is truly indescribable. It fills me with an overwhelming sense of pure love and connection to something greater than myself. To consciously experience the warmth of the sun, to see its brilliance with my inner eye, and to feel its gentle touch on my skin, represents a profound moment of connection with the Divine.

This gift of "seeing light" has brought me immense joy and a deep sense of gratitude for the extraordinary experiences I have been privileged to encounter. It serves as a reminder of the boundless love and presence of the Supreme Being in our lives, guiding us with light and warmth even in the darkest of times. However, at times, I couldn't help but wonder, "Why is this happening? Is my brain malfunctioning? I think not, but what is going on?" There's also the constant feeling of being "off," difficult to explain—almost as if I momentarily lose connection with earthly existence, adrift in space.

Sometimes, I feel strong vibrational energy working on my head, an intensity that makes me feel like pulling my hair out. I experience sensations of 'crawls,' movements resembling worms crawling from the top of my head down to my cheeks—quite unsettling. I remember seeking guidance from Swami-Gi (Himalayan Yoga & Meditation), my Guru, regarding these occurrences. "Is something wrong with my brain?" I asked. He assured me, "There's absolutely nothing wrong with your brain; it's your awareness that's expanding. You've been gifted with health; your purpose is to serve others."

I interpreted this as a sign that my gift of being cancer-free was meant for a greater purpose, urging me to realize my God-given potential. It awakened my awareness of other realms. Before this, my beliefs were shaped by my parents and earthly teachings: "All rivers flow into the same ocean," they'd say, emphasizing living well in every aspect of life. My mom's mantra was "Love is my religion," a motto I've adopted. While I believe in the evolution of the soul, I admit I was unfamiliar with spiritual dimensions. Initially, I viewed the world through a lens of negative forces, not recognizing the presence of benevolent ones around us.

Through my extensive visits to Casa Dom Inacio over the years, I've gained profound insights and developed a deep belief in the existence of benevolent forces surrounding us. Despite my previous hesitation and fearfulness, even knowing of my sister's gift for perceiving spiritual dimensions, my experiences have transformed my perspective.

After my trip to Casa Dom Inacio in 2007, I began to notice several significant changes, particularly in my awareness of mediumship and personal growth. I found myself sensing the emotions of others with increasing accuracy. At first, I resisted this, believing mediumship was only for those with psychic abilities. However, many people in this field commented on my growing mediumistic abilities, acknowledging their accelerated development. Eventually, I could no longer deny these experiences, especially after being recognized as clairsentient by Gail Thackray (Los Angeles Success Coach, Author, Speaker, and Psychic Healer).

Clairsentience, a psychic ability involving intuitive perception of energy, emotions, or spiritual information, became a part of my life unexpectedly. This gift allowed me to tune into the feelings and experiences of people, places, or situations on a deep, intuitive level. I often tested myself on accurately pinpointing others' emotions.

Another profound experience was seeing bright golden luminous lights frequently in the early hours of the morning. Living in the countryside of Stouffville, where it was dark with no nearby light sources, these lights appeared during a semi-conscious state. Feeling the sun's warmth on my face and seeing its brightness in my mind became a comforting presence, a sign of connection and reassurance during times of need.

Sometimes, bright lights resembling car headlights would appear, their luminosity and intensity so real that distinguishing between physical and spiritual reality became difficult. These experiences often startled me, especially when lights appeared unexpectedly and then vanished upon waking. Occasionally, lights appeared at my third eye, between my eyebrows, or lined paths with their brilliance.

In August 2007, on a beautiful full moon night in Abadiania near Casa Dom Inacio, I looked out my bedroom window to see a one to one-and-a-half-foot oblong golden yellow light in the direction of the moon. This sighting coincided with a period of struggling thoughts I had previously described.

Another memorable incident occurred on my birthday, a Wednesday, when I experienced the sun's flare on my closed eyelids during a sleep-wake state, despite the cloudy night. Days later, between four to five am, I witnessed an oblong shape surrounded by golden-white flames against a dark sky.

On September 26, 2010, a significant moment unfolded during my birthday celebration at the Vatican. It marked a thrilling occasion as my husband and I reunited after six years, overcoming the challenges of cancer, which had initially separated us due to healthcare needs. Living in different countries—Canada for accessible healthcare and Sacramento for my husband—our reunion in Chicago before flying to Rome on a Lufthansa plane promised excitement, romance, and cherished moments together.

We were staying in the smallest country in the world, the Vatican, spanning just one hundred and seven acres. It was thrilling to stay in a hotel at the Vatican bordering Italy, our room offering a view of the Basilica's dome. The sight was especially majestic at sunset, with the sun's rays casting vibrant colors on the dome, creating a superb spectacle. I recall my husband sitting silently on the balcony in his briefs, sipping a drink and gazing in awe at this magnificent sight.

On the night before my birthday, a Saturday night transitioning into Sunday morning, I was abruptly awakened from a deep sleep. I found myself touching my ears, attempting to stop the buzzing sound— "zzzzeeee", "zzzeeeeeee", "zzeeeeeeeee". The noise grew louder and louder, echoing in my ears and pounding in my eardrums. Concurrently, a deep, dark purple light appeared in the middle of my forehead, my third eye. The circular purple light expanded, swirling with increasing intensity, leaving me bewildered and disoriented. Glancing at the clock, I realized it was the early hours of my birthday morning. It dawned on me with profound clarity—this intense energy was a birthday gift from the Universe, a sign of grace and divine presence. I felt the vibrational strength of this energy and heard an inner voice affirming that I had received something special from the Universal Father. Overwhelmed with happiness and a deep sense of love, I embraced this moment of grace.

During another significant moment on a Thanksgiving weekend, just before falling asleep on a Sunday night, I witnessed a golden flame once more. This occurrence startled me because it typically happened in a semi-conscious state, not while drifting off to sleep. I saw a white box containing a bright flame, part of a series of light appearances that were becoming increasingly frequent. These experiences left me somewhat alarmed, questioning their connection to my spiritual evolution. Often, I would simply see a flame resembling a candle's glow. I soon realized these lights were gifts from the Entities of Light, aiding my spiritual growth and leaving me euphoric. I became consciously aware of being immersed in the light, engaging in inner dialogue about whether to stay immersed or return to the grounded reality of earthly life. Many times, I found myself so absorbed in the light that I suddenly realized my bladder was full, prompting me to rush to the bathroom.

During one Christmas season, I began seeing the colors of Christmas lights and images of deities. I vividly saw Mother Mary, feeling transported back to ancient times with her. This wasn't the first time I'd seen her in her youthful form. I also saw Indian deities, including Lord Shiva and baby Lord Krishna, often during meditation. These images appeared spontaneously, not as a result of deliberate thought. The lights manifested in various shapes—circles and oblongs—becoming a frequent occurrence. The oblong shape, in particular, appeared regularly, sometimes resembling a silver coin with intricate patterns. Once, while lying on my right side, a coin-shaped circle of light appeared very close to my face.

In 2019, I woke up to see myself peering through a tiny hole, witnessing a brilliant, piercing white light that momentarily blinded me with its glare. This intense light often started with a golden-white glow at the center of my forehead or third eye, gradually expanding and becoming more luminous. Simultaneously, I felt vibrational energy, often hearing a 'zoom, zoom' sound deep in my right ear. This sensation of pressure or fullness in my right ear became a normal occurrence over the years. The brightness of the light was so intense that it frequently woke me up between three to six am. In those moments of wakefulness, I felt incredibly alert, conscious, and filled with joy. However, as soon as I returned to ordinary reality, the light would vanish, leaving me enveloped in a profound sense of love.

Occasionally, a deep purple light would appear in a cylindrical shape, swirling and twirling in a mesmerizing dance. Drifting off to sleep, I would find myself captivated by the swirling motion of the purple light, accompanied by the gentle hum of vibrational energy.

These beautiful forms of energy and light became my friends. Surrounded by trees and untouched land cleared for housing, I became more attuned to the subtleties of other realms. During moments of solitude and anxiety, I felt accompanied by a loving force that communicated through the gentle glow of the sun on my face, often during the state between sleep and wakefulness. Sometimes, this light would manifest as a circular shape in the middle of my forehead.

I struggled with anxiety for decades, and the episodes were quite frightening. Trying to ward off the sensation of losing control of my senses was a constant effort. The fear of not being able to breathe or of fainting created a vicious cycle that required immense conscious effort to manage. Even now, I occasionally need to consciously employ my coping strategies. My spiritual practices became a crucial tool in gaining perspective and managing these feelings of being "out of control." During those challenging times, the presence of light helped me stay calm and kept the feeling of losing control in check.

My transformative journey to Abadiania, home of Casa Dom Inacio, proved to be a pivotal moment in my life, unlocking profound experiences and connections in the spiritual realm. Embracing exploration, I discovered the ability to perceive lights, orbs, and other ethereal wonders that had previously eluded me. These mystical encounters, combined with my dedication to spiritual growth, provided a grounding force that instilled deep confidence. I found solace in knowing that the Universal Father was intricately woven into the fabric of my existence, offering unwavering support precisely when I needed it most. This profound journey enriched my spiritual understanding and reaffirmed the profound significance of divine presence in my life.

Reflecting on my journey, I've realized that the 'Light' never left my side during times of isolation. It provided solace and comfort during moments of uncertainty and fear, becoming a constant presence that I deeply cherish. Imagining scenarios where urgent help was needed in the dead of night, with my husband thousands of miles away, it was the 'Light' that I could rely on. Its signs were unmistakable, repeatedly reassuring me of the watchful care and protection of the Divine. For this unwavering guidance and support, I am profoundly grateful.

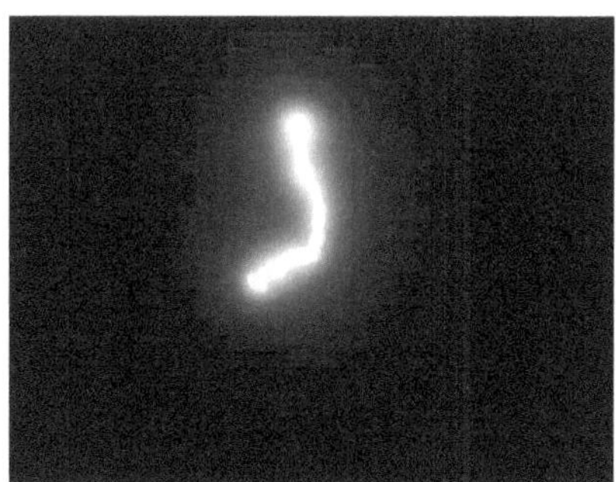 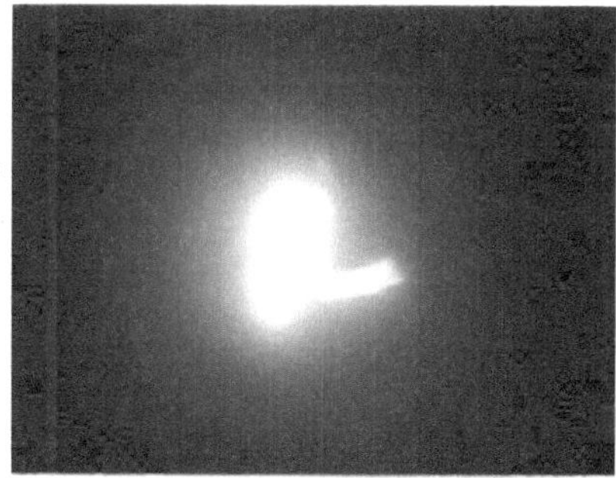

Figure 1&2 – energy forms taken from my camera on a full moon

Figure 3 - energy forms by the statute Santo Dom Inacio travelling towards Irma

Figure 4 – energy forms through Irma as she said a prayer to Santo Dom Inacio

Gifts Received – Seeing Orbs, Energies, Faces, and Eyes...

I am thrilled to share my experience with orbs. I first noticed these phenomena in my photos during my initial trip to Casa Dom Inacio in 2005. Orbs are often associated with spiritual beliefs and paranormal activities. In photography, orbs appear as circular artifacts captured in flash photography, believed to represent the energy of spirits or entities attempting to communicate with the living. They are said to manifest in places of positive energy, often during gatherings, conveying messages to both the photographer and those present in the photos. Personally, I've noticed that orbs seem to respond to our thoughts—when one seeks to capture them intentionally, they often elude capture.

A compelling read on orbs is "Orbs: Their Mission and Messages of Hope" by Klaus Heinemann, PhD, and Gundi Heinemann. Dr. Heinemann, a research professor at Stanford University, and his wife, a healing arts practitioner, provide interesting insights, confirming that orbs indeed represent spiritual energy with a mission to convey messages of hope. Their firsthand experiences with orbs near Casa Dom Inacio further underscore their significance.

During a June 2007 trip to Casa Dom Inacio, my friend Irma and I hurriedly made our way to the sacred waterfall, known locally as "cachoeira," one late afternoon around 5 pm. The setting sun cast a fiery glow over the landscape as we traversed the narrow, steep path from the waterfall. We paused to offer a prayer of gratitude to the Entities of Light before leaving, deciding to capture the glorious sunset with our old-fashioned cameras. Despite the unpredictable nature of orbs, they graced our photos abundantly that evening—appearing in vibrant hues of red, pale yellow, reddish-brown, and more. Some orbs even revealed faces, complete with tiny eyes and noses, creating a spectacular sight.

This charming story marks the beginning of my awareness of orbs and other energy forms. It all began during dinner at Dom Ingrid, my bed and breakfast (known as "pousada" in Portuguese), in 2007. I casually observed Irma rushing excitedly towards the entrance, typically a gathering place for guests from around the world, all seeking healing on various levels. Many ventured out into the darkness with cameras set to capture orbs using slow shutter speeds, hoping for remarkable sightings. Irma's unexpected announcement about a UFO show starting at 8 pm the following night left me skeptical, but I agreed to accompany her to humor her enthusiasm.

On the designated evening, as I savored dinner at the pousada, renowned for its local cuisine, Irma interrupted with her insistence on attending the UFO event. Reluctantly, I joined her, expecting little more than a quiet night under the vast, starlit sky overlooking the valley towards the cachoeira—the sacred waterfall. In those days, the area lacked urban development, with minimal lighting even at Casa Dom Inacio, contributing to the darkness that enveloped us. Suddenly, a light appeared above the waterfall, initially resembling a faint candle flame before growing brighter and larger. To my astonishment, the light divided into two, then four, and back to one, moving in a straight line before halting. We watched in silence, leaning against the veranda rails, apprehensive that any noise might disturb the scene. The display continued with lights growing brighter, occasionally joined by red ones that also divided and moved before vanishing abruptly by 9 pm, exactly as Irma predicted.

This event marked my introduction to witnessing these extraordinary energy forms. Initially overwhelming, these sightings soon became a regular occurrence in this unique setting. On that memorable evening, as I captured photos of the energy forms, a moment of startle overcame me—a sudden skip of my heartbeat—as I observed through my camera lens a golden flame-shaped orb seemingly moving towards me, resembling a head with discernible eyes. The unexpected encounter left me breathless and deeply moved.

As our evening drew to a close, we walked towards the statue of Santo Dom Inacio, where Irma typically offered a goodnight prayer. Sitting on a concrete bench nearby, I felt compelled to take a picture of her during her ritual. In those days, Casa Dom Inacio had minimal lighting. As I aimed my camera at Irma, who had her head bowed towards the statue, I noticed a strong white light on my camera screen. Three or four spots of light, seemingly from the sky, appeared—one passing directly through Irma's head. Another resembled a rope of electricity with what looked like a golden-colored bony hand. Astonished, I asked Irma to photograph me in the same location immediately afterward, but the lights had vanished, and nothing showed up on her camera. I am convinced these were Entities of Light, spiritual beings. It felt as though these events occurred at a time when I sought to restore my faith and manage my fears. This particular trip seemed to offer signs from the Entities of Light, providing proof to bolster my faith and strength.

On another occasion during Easter in 2009 at Casa Dom Inacio, I used a vintage compact camera to capture photos and was astonished by what appeared on the camera screen. Upon arriving at the Casa gates on the first evening of my trip, I snapped a few pictures. Thousands of orbs densely packed the frame, and in another photo, orbs were accompanied by four distinct lines resembling cords descending from above. Of course, there was no physical explanation for such lines or cords. As a newcomer to all of this, I eagerly captured images at the same spot sequentially. Many suggested these lines signified a connection to the heavens. I've included the photo I took at the end of this chapter for your viewing. The feeling of warmth and awe overwhelmed me, knowing that these spiritual beings were communicating with me, providing tangible proof of their presence.

Over the years, I have come across information regarding extraterrestrial theories, as discussed on shows like 'Ancient Aliens' and in news reports. Some of the phenomena mentioned, such as sightings reported by commercial pilots and others, resonate deeply with me because I have personally witnessed similar occurrences—shapes and sounds—in this off-the-grid area in Brazil. While I may not be an expert in this field, I can only share what I have seen with my own eyes. I have heard accounts from the people of Abadiania and visitors mentioning frequent UFO sightings in the area. Could it be true? Could there be some truth to these claims? All I know is that there must be something to it—there is nothing wrong with my eyesight. Indeed, extensive research has confirmed these sightings were genuine.

Another significant experience occurred in 2009 when I began seeing orbs with my naked eyes, often alongside radiant lights. The feeling of love and connection I experienced from witnessing these brilliant lights and orbs together was profound. Initially, I observed them mostly just before falling asleep, often accompanied by a vibrating 'zooming' sound and intense tingling sensations on my crown chakra, which soon became a norm. I began seeing formations like half-circles with white and golden hues, initially appearing on the left side of my vision—a prelude to another amazing gift I received. Lights would also manifest in the middle of my forehead, clearly visible through my third eye. Often, orbs appeared white at first, then intensified with flashes of golden hues. On some occasions, blue orbs appeared, known as master orbs, and I felt fortunate to capture a few photographs of them. Blue orbs are sometimes seen as a sign of heightened spiritual connection or awareness. My nephew, Sanjay, was born with this ability, often frightened by these orbs as a child. I vividly recall an incident when he, no more than seven or eight years old, spent a night with me in the suburbs and exclaimed, "Auntie, there's a huge yellow circle of light over your picture on the wall." It became a regular occurrence for him, and I, mindful not to cause alarm, casually inquired about his perception of the orbs, treating it as a commonplace event. Decades later, I stand here, now decades his senior, privileged to witness these orbs firsthand—a testament to life's ongoing mysteries and wonders. The orbs I see have grown increasingly vivid and tangible, lingering fully formed for extended periods. These ethereal manifestations now grace me not only during moments of wakeful awareness but also at various times throughout the day. The light emanates with clarity, whether appearing at the center of my forehead or dancing at the edge of my vision. As I write, a fiery golden orb catches my gaze, illuminating the depths of my left eye with its mesmerizing presence. Each sighting fills me with wonder and a profound sense of connection to something greater than myself.

FACES & EYES

I believe it was around 2010 when I began seeing faces and eyes. Initially, I was frightened because I couldn't comprehend what was happening. "How on earth am I seeing these things now?" I asked myself. I had heard of other planets, different planes of existence, dimensions, and communicating with spirit beings, but experiencing it myself was beyond belief. These faces—my goodness—some had enormous teeth, others were just ugly, with huge eyes staring back at me. I had never seen these faces in my reality before. They appeared as I was about to fall asleep or in a state between sleep and wakefulness.

When discussing this with others who had more knowledge of such phenomena, they suggested I might be connecting to another realm or in touch with another world—how eerie. I would see eyes, sometimes just eyes, either two eyes or just one, looking directly at me. These eyes resembled those depicted in pictures of Tibet. Many structures in Tibet have an eye fixed atop them as part of their architecture. Sometimes during my early morning meditations, I would briefly see an eye—just one—appear between my eyebrows, at my third eye. It would last a few seconds before disappearing. I grew accustomed to seeing these eyes; sometimes they seemed to communicate, though remembering their messages, or understanding them was a challenge.

I felt as though 'something' was guiding me, connected to a wisdom beyond my own. I recall one instance where an eye seemed to communicate telepathically, mentioning that someone had gone to heaven for two weeks, suggesting an out-of-body experience, with the person due to return "here" on Earth in two weeks. While I didn't fully grasp the meaning, the telepathic communication felt special.

Over the years, I've grown less fearful of these faces. No matter how unsettling they may appear, I acknowledge them with a smile and continue with my sleep. Sometimes I see babies; their faces seem familiar yet not from this lifetime or world. On an early morning in April 13, 2014, I saw myself carrying a beautiful baby girl. Her legs were wrapped around my waist as I perused a line of fresh fruits, each vividly colored. The large strawberries, halved, were a striking vibrant red. The baby girl herself appeared vivid, with curly blond hair and crystal-clear eyes that looked almost like glass, a mesmerizing blue. I wondered who this baby could be. I recalled another incident during a prior trip in 2010, from Venice to Switzerland. I was asleep on our coach when I was awakened by the presence of a beautiful baby girl beside me, also blond with curly hair. It felt so real that it took me some time to readjust to reality. The baby's presence startled me; could she be a child from a past or future life? At other times, I've seen unsettling images, like that of a dead baby with sunken eyes staring back at me, prompting me to urge someone to release the spirit.

Eyes have also appeared in other instances, such as when I bowed before the statue of Santo Dom Ignacio and felt an eye staring back at me. I've noticed that when I'm with someone to whom I feel a special connection, I often see faces associated with that person's nationality. One person dear to me, whom my husband and I affectionately call "our South African daughter," Mpumi, has been a catalyst for such encounters. Whenever I'm around her, I often sense the presence of various black faces—of all kinds and shapes—whom I haven't encountered in this lifetime. I believe they are trying to communicate with me, though deciphering their message remains a challenge.

Throughout my journeys to Abadiania, home of Casa Dom Inacio, I've encountered extraordinary experiences. The Entities of Light, manifesting through the Medium, have offered healing and guidance to countless people worldwide. It feels like a privilege to have witnessed such profound events in my lifetime. Visiting this sacred place felt like an invitation from the Entities of Light themselves, with every step aligning seamlessly. The surreal yet tangible nature of these events has strengthened my belief in miracles. I am grateful for the opportunities to strengthen my faith, practice forgiveness, and discover the essence of true love by tapping into my inner power.

Through my experiences, I hope to convey the message that "LOVE" is the ultimate answer. May my stories inspire you to embrace the power of love and recognize the miracles that exist within and around us.

Figure 1 – An Orb shower with lines on the far right

Figure 2 – At sunrise, Master Orbs

Figure 3 – A Brazilian visiting tribe – happy orbs

Figure 4 – At sunrise – Orbs surrounding my brother

Figure 5 – Sunrise by the Casa, orbs surrounding Natalia and I

Tools to Aid on the Journey to Accessing LOVE Within

Summary Chapter
Tools to Aid on the Journey to Accessing LOVE Within

To my cherished readers, I humbly offer a glimpse into the sacred tools that have guided me on my ongoing quest to forge a profound bond with the Universal Father. May these insights serve as beacons of light as you navigate the depths of your own inner odyssey. Embrace your imperfections, for within them lies the essence of perfection.

The following are routines I embraced to develop my "Connection to Spirit" muscle before illness:

- I delved into the teachings of Kriya Yoga, introduced to the West by Paramahansa Yogananda, known as the "Father of Yoga in the West." I was drawn to the bridge between Eastern and Western religions, finding balance between Western material growth and Indian spirituality. Attending Sunday sessions, I cherished the community united by this bridge.

- Hatha yoga, focusing on the science of breath, held a special allure for me. Its origins traced back generations to a man who introduced yoga to my home country, Guyana. As an adult in Toronto, I formed a deep bond with my Himalayan Yoga and Meditation guru, known affectionately as my spiritual grand-daughter. I cherished our time together during his trips to Toronto, where I was lovingly dubbed the 'tea girl.' I found profound beauty in the unity of Christians, Buddhists, Zoroastrians, and other faiths gathering around the message of "All About Love."

- Focusing on breath was transformative; Hatha yoga helped me transition from chest breathing to deeper, diaphragmatic breathing, alleviating anxieties caused by various stresses.

- Prayers, Yoga, and Meditation are my tools; they may not be yours. Find what resonates, stirs your heartstrings, and invokes a love within that defies words. Spiritual practices can include chanting, contemplative walks, or listening to waves crashing along the shore—as long as you connect with the Silence within.

- Volunteering, giving service to others, was impactful for me. Devoting hours weekly to a Tae Kwon Do club—from office paperwork to cleaning toilets to sparring with kids—often left me physically bruised but deeply fulfilled by the opportunity to shape young lives.

- Volunteering at the CVICU (Cardio Vascular Intensive Care Unit) was profoundly rewarding, allowing me to express gratitude to the place that saved my father's life. Bringing comfort to families awaiting news of loved ones undergoing heart surgeries through simple gestures like offering a smile filled me with fulfillment. This experience was truly a 'Win-Win,' strengthening my spirit while allowing me to give back meaningfully.

- -The Mirror Technique—a daily practice of looking at your reflection and seeing yourself. Reflecting on "Who is 'I'?" and acknowledging the divine love within, recognizing that we are made in God's image, with "royal blood running through our veins" (Pastor Joel Osteen). Offering a high-five or saying "I love you" to oneself became a powerful practice.

- Forgiveness—an essential tool that requires courage to forgive oneself or others before moving forward. Through the process of "Finding Your Power Within," I found the strength to release burdens and experience a profound sense of relief.

As I share my personal journey, I hope it resonates with you, inspiring you to discover and embrace your own tools that deeply resonate with your being. Transformation is gradual, requiring time, repetition, persistence, and unwavering consistency. Through dedicated practice, these tools integrate into your essence, becoming second nature. This internalization is crucial, ensuring that during life's challenges, our innate strength emerges effortlessly. Personally, without this foundation, I question whether I would have navigated a cancer diagnosis coinciding with my wedding period.

The following are things I routinely did to reboot and enhance my "Connection to Spirit" after illness:

Maintaining Self-Love

When I was diagnosed, my family and I were shocked! I had been eating the right foods, taking my vitamins, and preparing for my Black Belt and a new chapter as a bride. Without the foundation of 'Self Love,' I couldn't have managed as well as I am now. At that time, I felt broken on every level—mind, body, and spirit—all of which needed a boost.

I felt numb for a while, especially during chemotherapy. I yearned to reconnect with the Heavenly Father. Though I had felt the presence of something greater before my illness, during and after surgery, I sometimes felt emotionally numb. I revisited the tools I had relied upon in the past to rediscover my sense of self. My spiritual connection became more profound and precise, as if the Universe guided me along a challenging path to clarify my life's purpose. Now, I firmly believe that the dreams planted in my heart and my mission in this lifetime have become crystal clear.

Yoga and meditation became precise, focused practices, forming consistent habits now part of my daily routine.

- I was drawn to an extraordinary place pulsating with intense energy, where miracles, including my own, are said to occur. This secluded sanctuary in Brazil deeply resonates with my spirit, its call unmistakable—as if I were being led there, guided along a perfectly crooked path.

- Embracing Persistence and Consistency: I dedicate tranquil early morning hours, one and a half to two hours before the demands of the workday, to nurturing the 'Self.' This ritual anchors me, tailored to suit my needs. Your journey may take a different form; the key is discovering what resonates with your essence.

I tapped into the power of the following tools to rebuild and revitalize myself:

- Gratitude Journal: Each day, I took time to jot down a few things I was grateful for, fostering a positive mindset.

- Dream Journal: Recognizing the potential for spiritual insights during sleep, I made it a habit to record my dreams upon waking, allowing for deeper reflection.
- Yoga: Embracing the unity of mind, body, and spirit, I engaged in physical postures to prepare for meditation, seeking inner stillness and balance.
- Affirmations: By vocalizing positive affirmations, I harnessed the mind's ability to manifest reality, reinforcing self-belief and motivation.
- Visualization: Firmly believing in its power, I consistently used visualization techniques to achieve milestones such as obtaining my CPA designation during my career journey.
- Prayers and Meditation: I love to pray out loud, feeling a connection to someone or something listening. Engaging in conversations with the Universe brings me great satisfaction, as I truly believe it listens—an analogy you can test through a small experiment to experience its efficacy.
- Walking alongside Water, Listening to Nature: I find solace in walking alongside water, listening to birds or ducks, and motivational tapes.
- Spirit Spot: I found mine in Brazil. Where is yours?
- Crystal Bed: Designed by Divine Light Beings, this method uses light and crystals for vibrational healing across all levels of body, mind, and spirit.

Healing energy pulses through the body's energy field, including the seven main chakra centers.

- Reiki Practice: A form of energy healing where universal energy is transferred through the palms. As a second-level initiate, I sometimes use this method.

Establishing a consistent practice was the lifeline that saved me. Discovering profound love within and engaging with my inner voice—a force greater than myself—was transformative. Engaging in spiritual practices kept me rooted and centered, expanding my awareness and unveiling invaluable gifts along the way.

This is my message to you: **<u>LOVE yourself!</u> This is the key to self-esteem and confidence, making us less dependent on others for happiness.** Loving ourselves exactly as we are, with our imperfections, is crucial. We are beautiful in our uniqueness, made in the image of our most High God. We are special, we are loved! **We** are the power! This message is vital; our thoughts define us. Thoughts are powerful, our spiritual food. **"I AM"** the answer to my thoughts!

I love YOU!

Figure 1 - Benji having a Crystal Bed session
(blessed crystals along the chakra points)

Figure 2 – with my brother, sis & Medium Joao

Figure 3- Sunrise by the Casa, capturing
Loving Energies

BONUS CHAPTER

Power Together

Dear readers, it is with immense joy and deep affection that I introduce you to two kindred spirits who hold a special place in my heart. Each of them has graciously contributed a chapter, revealing the essence of their world and the profound truth that 'LOVE' is indeed the answer. Please, immerse yourself and enjoy their heartfelt stories in the following two chapters.

CHAPTER TEN

The Power of Sharing Stories by Mpumi Nobiva

I believe in the power of sharing personal narratives because I have seen it work and transform my own life. I was born on January 8, 1993, into the oppression of abject poverty in South Africa and orphaned soon after, at the age of nine, when my mother died of AIDS. We lived in a corrugated tin shack housing more than nine family members in a township called Zonkizizwe, located in Katlehong, Johannesburg. When I was born, my father was 22 years old and my mother 17 years old. My father did not stick around long enough to watch me crawl, and my mother did not live long enough to experience most of my childhood. While absent throughout my life, I recognize the two greatest gifts they offered me: a life of unique experiences and deep abandonment wounds to heal; opportunities to embody a new story.

As an infant, I lived in post-apartheid South Africa where townships were vibrant with a juxtaposition of optimism and violence. As the new 'Rainbow Nation' democracy-led South Africa emerged, it ushered in tribal conflicts since native (black) people could now compete for national positions of political power. This riveting transformation took historic form as the democratic election of President Nelson Mandela in 1994. Albeit a great turning point in our history, there were unfortunate conflicts that ensued as a result of ethno-political struggles for power in many South African townships, and Zonkizizwe was one of them.

I am told by my 85-year-old beloved grandmother, Ntombise Vivian Nobiva, that the violence resulting from the ethno-political conflict became so much that we had to flee, leaving the little we had behind, and seek refuge in the southern suburbs of Rosettenville (Johannesburg South). In our early years in Rosettenville, I was raised by my grandmother, a domestic worker who had nine children, and we lived with my grandfather, who fixed cars. I was born an only child but raised as my grandparents' last born with a couple of my aunts and uncles standing in as older siblings while my 20-year-old young mother braved the heart of Johannesburg Central Business District trying to earn a living and support me, her only child. As a result, she was rarely with the family.

I am told that she tried many different kinds of jobs to no long-term success as she had not completed her high school education. She worked as a security guard, and after becoming unemployed, she became a hairstylist. From there, she went to work at a food market, and after being let go, she lived with friends and began working as a prostitute on the streets of Johannesburg. This is where she would contract the Human Immunodeficiency Virus (HIV).

Before my mother was sick, she would visit on some weekends, and these would be the best days of my life. She would bring clothes from the city that none of my friends could copy and would braid my hair into the most beautiful styles imaginable; therefore, her absence did not really affect me. My grandmother, throughout our struggles with poverty, made sure that I never went a single night without being fed. Although our life was different, I always understood clearly that I was loved by the women who raised me.

Life continued in this manner until I was approximately eight, and for the first time, my mother came home and stayed longer than usual. I started noticing that a massive rash was breaking out all over her body; she started to shed massive amounts of her body weight and was always coughing. At first, she had the rash; then a flu; then it was Tuberculosis (TB); then she was admitted into the hospital for long periods of time as her condition would worsen. One day I would come home and my mother would be back from the hospital; the next, she would be gone again.

I remember returning from school one day to find my frail mother sitting alone on her bed, deep in thought. As I walked in, she slowly raised her head, invited me to join her, and, for the first time, she shared her personal story with me. She told me that she had made many mistakes in her life and did not want me to make the same mistakes: "Mama is HIV positive, and I don't ever want you to end up like me because I am sick and will soon die." I remember listening to her and feeling weakened with fear, my heart banging hard against my chest.

Although I did not completely understand what being HIV positive meant, I knew it was not good, and I also knew that Mama said that she will soon die. I honestly do not remember most of what she said after uttering the words "I will soon die," but I do remember her cupping my face with her soft hand, looking me straight in my eyes, and saying, "Do not be afraid, my baby; you will turn out fine; just promise me that you will be good to Gogo [a Nguni term meaning granny]. Promise me that you will do your best in school and that you will never stop believing in God." There was a moment of peace as our eyes met, and I tearfully nodded in agreement and quietly whispered, "I promise." She was 25 years old, and I was only 9, but both of us were able to connect as one through the power of personal sharing.

My mother giving a piece of herself to me is by far the greatest love I have encountered—her courage to openly expose a truth so cutting and, in the same breath, expressing her hopes and dreams for my future. Her narrative inspired me to believe that her departure was no reason to give up on life. That gifting of her truth is what brought a sense of peace and calmness into my life as the family and I began to face the wrath of living with an HIV-positive loved one. For 18 months, I painfully observed my mother's transition into full-blown AIDS: losing most of her hair, her skin tone turning darker and darker, her eyes sucked into their sockets, lips rip with open sores, and her chest and rib bones poking out.

I remember at some point I was told I could no longer kiss her or share any food or liquids with her. This broke my heart because I loved being close to her. Although weak, on some days she would get violent hallucinations of someone trying to kill her and hang halfway out of our bathroom window screaming; on other days, she would be so weak that she would just lay in bed helplessly, crying and wincing from the pain she was in. My mother was pronounced dead at around 7:30 on Thursday morning, June 2, 2002, as I was on my way to school.

Unlike most members of my family and the majority of South Africans at the time, I was never afraid to speak openly about how my mother died and that she died of AIDS-related complications. Alas, I do not blame any of the people who are or were ashamed because HIV and AIDS was and is still taboo in many parts of South Africa and Africa. According to the AIDS Foundation of South Africa, "Sub-Saharan Africa is the region worst-affected by HIV and AIDS [and] a prominent health concern; South Africa has the highest prevalence of HIV/AIDS compared to any other country in the world with 7.7 million people living with HIV, and 240,000 HIV-related deaths recorded in 2018" ("UNAIDS").

I confidently look back to my struggles with poverty and as an AIDS orphan with great compassion and gratitude. I believe that my mother's truth saved me from falling into the same life pattern because South Africa still battles with the same, arguably worse, socio-economic issues that also impacted my mother during her time as a young woman. Issues of crime, poverty, lack of adequate health care, inadequate access to education, lack of social security, and government corruption reinforcing unrest still exist within a very patriarchal society where young women are the first to fall through the cracks. Women face a greater risk of infection, with an average of three women infected with HIV for every two men who are infected; to make matters worse, but not completely surprising, "the difference is greatest in the 15-25 age group, where three young women for every one young man are infected," because their voices are the least heard—which is why young South African women especially must tell their stories ("HIV/AIDS in South Africa").

Today, I recognize and own the power of my narrative. As a 31-year-old, I share my story as a motivational speaker to inspire other orphans; people affected by HIV and AIDS, young women (South African, African, and anywhere else in the world), people who live in poverty, women who are still oppressed, and many others—to help them realize that they are more than their circumstances. They are more than the initial hardship highlighted in their life stories.

Every time I share with others my personal narrative, my own tragic experiences, I repeatedly inspire others, and I am constantly reminded of who I am and what my power is. Colum McCann, National Book Award-winning novelist, Narrative 4 cofounder, and one of my main inspirations, says, "Our stories are the glue of what we are. They stitch together what we become. Our ability to tell them is fundamental to how we celebrate and examine our lives." Through our stories, we create and shape who we are and who we get to be during our time on this earth. The teller is both a presenter and an audience; both a teller and a listener; both vulnerable and healer. I believe it is the art that captures on the canvas of life the true meaning behind why we are here.

The journey and inquiry of personal storytelling have been a very personal unfolding for me. I started sharing my story while I was a student at The Oprah Winfrey Leadership Academy for Girls in South Africa. I was 17 years old at a World AIDS Day conference in 2010 when something inside of me shook awake in dissatisfaction as I observed how the conference shared and focused on the mainstream narrative about HIV/AIDS: statistics, prevention measures, sexual education, etc., but nothing related to telling actual stories of people like my mother, and naming them. People like myself who have been orphaned as a result, who also have names and stories to tell.

I knew then as a student, who also had the added advantage of experiencing the AIDS epidemic, that it was not enough to focus only on facts that speak to people's minds and neglect the stories which open the heart. I wondered how ignorant members in our community would understand that HIV/AIDS does not discriminate and can infect anyone who is exposed, regardless of age, gender, race, or even lifestyle as many people assumed. I spoke up, and my life was never the same. I felt like a cap had opened in me, and like I was breathing for the first time. I realize now that what I experienced was the healing power of sharing my story and its powerful grace, which restores me as I am once again reconnected with the community and seen for my personal truth. This is a liberation like no other, and I wanted it for others as well.

The wheels of my storytelling journey began to turn, and I grew into a stronger and more visible speaker as I was blessed with many opportunities to travel and share my story with different people and communities in my country and beyond. I excelled in the first class of the Oprah Winfrey Leadership Academy for Girls in South Africa before coming to the United States to study. I spoke everywhere, and anywhere that people would listen to how the power of sharing personal stories can change and improve lives.

Thanks to Mom Oprah (Ms. Oprah Winfrey), I was able to speak at the White House, congressional fundraisers, corporate functions, and nonprofit initiatives in several countries. I now hold a master's degree in Strategic Communications from High Point University and serve as the first alumnus on the Board of Directors of the Oprah Winfrey Leadership Academy for Girls in South Africa. My official, public title became: award-winning international speaker and communication strategist. I began organizing and initiating social development programs in South Africa and moved to Los Angeles to join a leadership software development company, NationBuilder, where I was the first Leader in Residence developing the digital infrastructure for Share Your Story Africa—an initiative inspired by our advocacy work uniting youth against HIV/AIDS and domestic violence in South Africa—all while sharing my story at events around the world. I also became experienced in hosting events and facilitating workshops.

It was on the heels of one of these unforgettable life moments of traveling, connecting, and sharing that I met my darling angel Satie, who has since become like a mother and mentor alike. She opened her heart so selflessly to my wonder and desire to explore the world of healing even deeper—hosting me several times at her serene healing condo in Toronto as well as in her lovely home in Las Vegas. I learned a lot about the miraculous experience she manifested in healing herself and bringing it to world stages to bless many others. Proving yet again, the power of our humanity and how it extended across all of our destined life paths, the straightforward and crooked. All perfect nonetheless.

Mpumi Nobiva, M.A,. Strategic Communications, International Speaker, Artist and Rise Mzansi Provincial Legislature and National Assembly Candidate
Website: https:/ mpuminobiva.com/
LinkedIn: https://www.linkedin.com/in/mpuminobiva/

CHAPTER ELEVEN

It's All About Love by Jessica York

L ove is a tricky thing, isn't it? It is not always automatic. It doesn't always come easy. But it IS the most wonderful thing in the world. And the easiest way to access it is by choosing it! Love is a choice, a choice to give and to receive. And yet, it is the formless, invisible, tasteless, odorless, soundless energy that creates and sustains life.

I started my journey on earth with a jolt of harsh reality. When I was just days old, I was taken from my mother's arms—the only thing my five senses knew at the time—and given to two excited, love-filled, eager parents, thus blessing me with the "primal wound."

First, let me explain the theory of the "primal wound." The term was coined in the essay *Adoption: The Primal Wound Effects of Separation from the Birth Mother on

Adopted Children* by Nancy Verrier, M.A. In a nutshell, Verrier suggests that for love to be freely accepted, there must be trust, and despite the love and security adoptive parents give, adopted kids suffer from constant anxiety, wondering when they will be rejected again. So, they tend to reject before they can be rejected. Verrier proposes that for an adopted child, allowing oneself to love and be loved is too dangerous because they cannot trust that they will not be abandoned again. So, why would I say blessed by the primal wound? Because living with and overcoming this distrust and anxiety (which has given me a Master's level education in the power of love, especially self-love) allowed me to succeed in a career in television (one that is filled with constant rejection) and has become the basis of what I teach at Broadcast Like a Badass. To equip me in teaching the power of self-love, the Universe didn't just give me a primal wound; it doubled down.

My adopted parents divorced when I was seven. They both remarried: my dad to a woman with two daughters, creating a perceived Cinderella story for me, and my mom to a man who she would, despite his abusive outbursts, choose to defend rather than protect her two small children. To say I questioned the existence of love (especially unconditional love) during the first thirty-five years of my life is an understatement. But as I stated before, love is a tricky thing.

When Satie asked me to do a chapter in her book, I was first honored, and then imposter syndrome kicked in… What did I know about love? I started to think about the definition of love. I even turned to my BFFs Oxford, Webster, and Google for a little wise counsel. There are so many definitions of love! As a noun, according to the Oxford dictionary, it is an "intense feeling of affection," "a great interest and pleasure in something," or a "personified figure of love," often represented as Cupid. As a verb, it is to "feel deep affection for someone" or "like or enjoy very much." The Internet told me that love came from an old English term *lufu*, which was of Germanic origin; from an Indo-European root shared by Sanskrit *lubhyati* 'desires,' Latin *libet* 'it's pleasing,' and *libido* 'desire.' But for me, love seems way more complicated and simple at the same time.

To boil it down—love creates, and a lack of love destroys. When I learned that choosing to love myself created possibilities, happiness, stability, harmony, and love all around, I finally understood what unconditional love meant. Although I'm not a specifically religious person (meaning I don't subscribe to one particular religion; I identify more as a spiritual aficionado), I do find immense wisdom in the 1 Corinthians 13:4-8 scripture where it says, *"Love is patient, love is kind. It does not envy, it does not boast, it is not proud. It does not dishonor others, it is not self-seeking, it is not easily angered, it keeps no records of wrongs. Love does not delight in evil but rejoices with the truth. It always protects, always trusts, always hopes, always perseveres. Love never fails."*

When I was young, I always thought that when I found love, the above is what it would look like. However, as my life experiences have taught me, I realize that is not true at all. This is who you need to BE if you want to have love be present in your life. Breaking this wisdom down, I have come to not just believe but know to my core that: Love is patient—you need to exercise patience when a situation arises where choosing patience would bring love to life. Love is kind—you need to choose kindness when a situation arises where you have the choice to respond with kindness or hatred. Choose kindness over selfishness. Choose kindness over jealousy, etc. When we choose kindness, we bring love to life. It does not envy, it does not boast, it is not proud—when you choose to turn that kindness on yourself and love yourself, there is no need to be envious, boastful, or proud. You know your self-worth. You are not in competition with anyone else. You do not need to be envious of what anyone else has because you are perfect. You love yourself AS IS. You are whole and complete. You don't need to tell anyone about how worthy you are, because their opinion of you has no influence on your self-worth. You love yourself completely.

Here is the kicker about self-love. If you don't love yourself completely—AS IS, you won't be able to believe anyone else can love you either. And therefore, you will always be rejecting someone's love. Because obviously, if you can't love yourself, who else could?! Trust me, I have years of experience doing this. Going back to the description of the primal wound from above, decades of rejecting others before they could reject me got me nowhere. Once I understood that at the core of it all was my own self-rejection.

Once I chose to love and accept myself, AS IS, I realized that no one could take that away from me and I became rejection-proof. It does not dishonor others—when life asks you to tear people down to build yourself up, love reminds you that that is unnecessary because your self-worth is in competition with no one. It is not self-seeking—love means operating out of an abundance mindset, and therefore you are not self-seeking. When you operate out of love, there is plenty enough to go around. That's why they say sharing is caring. It is not easily angered—when love is present and you are operating from a place of kindness, with a solid dose of patience, believing you are worthy, not in comparison or competition with anyone, it is very hard to get mad at anyone. It keeps no records of wrongs—when you stop bringing up a laundry list of someone else's wrongdoings, when you forgive, let go, and just focus on the present moment issue (with kindness and patience), you feel more love. Love does not delight in evil but rejoices with the truth—do you know what is an instant relationship killer? Lying! Do you know what builds strength in relationships? The truth! So often we tell white lies because we don't think our truth is strong enough (we don't see our worthiness) and we are afraid we will be rejected if we tell our truth. But telling our truth is a huge form of self-love. You are worthy as is! And so is your truth. It always protects, always trusts, always hopes, always perseveres—when you protect your self-worth, trust your self-worth, hope for the best because you choose to see the kindness in others and are patient enough to let them show it to you (and you recognize it because you're not focused on all their wrongdoings), LOVE is what you feel. When you bring love to the table, you always persevere. It's true.

Love never fails, especially self-love because that is the only love we can truly control. Love grows things. That's why so often it is compared to light and the creator. A lack of love or darkness kills. The choice is really black and white, light and dark. What will you choose? I choose life. I choose love.

Jessica York, CEO Won World Productions, Inc., Chief Badass at Broadcast Like a Badass, Emmy Nominated Host, Producer and Red Carpet Reporter.

If you choose to continue the conversation, please connect with me at www.jessyork.com
http://www.broadcastlikeabadass.com/

ABOUT THE AUTHORS

Satie Narain-Simon is a Chartered Professional Accountant (CPA) who has made a remarkable 180% shift from a two plus decade career as a corporation tax auditor for the Canadian government to passionately advocating for the transformative power of self-discovery and LOVE.

Satie is a co-author, international speaker, coach, and a dedicated volunteer. She is a practitioner of Reiki, holds a Black Stripe in Tae-Kwon Do, and a 'Daughter' at the House of the Casa Dom Inacio, Brazil. As an initiate of Swami Veda Bharati's lineage within the Himalayan tradition of Yoga and Meditation, she integrates these profound practices into her work.

Her volunteer efforts include serving on the Waterfront Magazine Planning Committee and judging for the Canadian International Films for Peace and the BIFF.

Through her varied roles and relentless enthusiasm, Satie continues to advocate for kindness and inspire others to embark on their own journeys of self-discovery and fulfillment. Her story is one of resilience, transformation, and unwavering commitment to making the world a better place through the power of LOVE.

Proudly Guyanese, with a rich Caribbean cultural background, Satie currently lives in Toronto, Canada, and Las Vegas, USA.

If you would like to book Satie to speak at your next event, please visit:

Email: satiesimon@gmail.com
LinkedIn: https://www.linkedin.com/in/satie-narain-simon-20ab5a135
Facebook: https://www.facebook.com/satienarain

A w a r d - W i n n i n g International Speaker and Communication Strategist Mpumi Nobiva, has spoken at the White House, congressional fundraisers, corporate functions and nonprofit initiatives in several countries. She excelled in the first class of the Oprah Winfrey Leadership Academy for Girls in South Africa before coming to the United States to study. She currently holds a master's degree in Strategic Communications from High Point University, USA and served as the first alumnus on the Board of Directors of the Oprah Winfrey Leadership Academy for girls in South Africa.

Mpumi lives between Johannesburg and Cape Town, South Africa where she consults in narrative storytelling work and practices healing arts through creative work which she finds healing for her childhood trauma. Her personal struggles of surviving what it means to be who she is - is now the unique currency she transmutes in the name of service, healing and transformation. Her struggles have formed connecting bridges of hope to communities she represents and serves in South Africa's national political landscape as Rise Mzansi's Candidate for Provincial Legislature & The National Assembly.

Website: https://mpuminobiva.com/
LinkedIn: https://www.linkedin.com/in/mpuminobiva/

Meet Jessica York, the daringly adventurous, delightfully witty Emmy-Nominated TV host and producer! From her start as an intrepid investigative reporter in her very own series, "What's for Dinner, Ma?" to thrilling roles at MTV News, HGTV, and more, Jessica's media journey has been as diverse as it is dynamic.

She's dived with sharks, swam alongside elephants, and raced cars with the likes of Paul Newman—all in a day's work! Whether fronting CNN Headline News' Outdoor Update or captivating audiences with her Emmy-nominated travel show, "Hot Spots," Jessica's career has been a whirlwind of excitement.

As a seasoned host of GSN's Quiz Nation, Play Mania, and 100 Winners, and Rachael Ray's trusted travel expert, she's graced screens with her infectious energy and expertise. For over a decade, Jessica's been a staple on Dish Network, anchoring news and dazzling on red carpets.

During the pandemic, Jessica turned her focus to empowering others, coaching the camera-shy to shine with confidence and charisma. When she's not globe-trotting or coaching thought leaders, you'll find her teaching yoga on sandy shores, baking killer cupcakes, or carving up slopes on her snowboard.

Jessica York: Where adventure meets entertainment, and every moment sparkles with her signature charm!

www.jessyork.com

Did this book resonate with you?

Your thoughts mean the world to me! Every single review makes a huge difference and helps spread the message of finding strength within.

🌟 **Leave a Review!** 🌟

If you enjoyed this journey, I'd be thrilled if you could take a moment to share your experience. Head over to Amazon, or wherever you bought this book, and leave your honest review. Your feedback not only helps others discover these pages but also fuels my passion for writing and sharing.

From the bottom of my heart, thank you for being a part of this journey. Your support, enthusiasm, and insights are what keep me going. I'm endlessly grateful for your time, your thoughts, and for allowing my words to be a part of your life.

Thank you, thank you, thank you!

With love,

Katie ♡

July 2024

RESOURCES

The Miracle Man – The Life Story of Joao De Deus - Robert Pellegrino-Estrich

Orbs – Their Mission and Messages of Hope –Klaus Heinemann, PhD, & Gundi Heinemann

The Book Of Miracles – The Healing Work of Joao de Deus – Josie RavenWing

NOSSO LAR – Life in The Spirit World – Francisco Candido Xavier Dictated by the spirit Andre Luiz

Referenced Joel Osteen – USA pastor

Google

Referenced Tony Robbins

Motivational Podcasts by Dr. Wayne Dyer

Satesh Narain - www.casasdehealing.com

About Defining Moments Press

Built for aspiring authors who are looking to share transformative ideas with others throughout the world, Defining Moments Press offers life coaches, healers, business professionals, and other non-fiction or self-help authors a comprehensive solution to getting their books published without breaking the bank or taking years. Defining Moments Press prides itself on bringing readers and authors together to find tools and solutions.

As an alternative to self-publishing or signing with a major publishing house, we offer full profits to our authors, low-priced author copies, and simple contract terms.

Most authors get stuck trying to navigate the technical end of publishing. The comprehensive publishing services offered by Defining Moments Press mean that your book will be designed by an experienced graphic artist, available in printed, hard copy format, and coded for all eBook readers, including the Kindle, iPad, Nook, and more.

We handle all the technical aspects of your book creation so you can spend more time focusing on your business that makes a difference for other people.

Defining Moments Press founder, publisher, and #1 bestselling author Melanie Warner has over 20 years of experience as a writer, publisher, master life coach, and accomplished entrepreneur.

You can learn more about Warner's innovative approach to self-publishing or take advantage of free training and education at: MyDefiningMoments.com.

DEFINING MOMENTS BOOK PUBLISHING

If you're like many authors, you have wanted to write a book for a long time, maybe you have even started a book … but somehow, as hard as you have tried to make your book a priority, other things keep getting in the way.

Some authors have fears about their ability to write or whether anyone will value what they write or buy their book. For others, the challenge is making the time to write their book or having accountability to finish it.

It's not just finding the time and confidence to write that is an obstacle. Most authors get overwhelmed with the logistics of finding an editor, finding a support team, hiring an experienced designer, and figuring out all the technicalities of writing, publishing, marketing, and launching a book. Others have written a book and might have even published it but did not find a way to make it profitable.

For more information on how to participate in our next Defining Moments Author Training program, visit www.MyDefiningMoments.com
Or
email support@MyDefiningMoments.com

The Beauty of Change: The Fun Way for Women to Turn Pain Into Power & Purpose—Jean Amor Ramoran

From No Time to Free Time: 6 Steps to Work/Life Balance for Business Owners—Christoph Nauer

Self-Healing for Sexual Abuse Survivors: Tired of Just Surviving, Time to Thrive—Nickie V. Smith

Prepared Bible Study Lessons: Weekly Plans for Church Leaders—John W. Warner

Frog on a Lily Pad—Michael Lehre

How to Effectively Supercharge Your Career as a CEO—Giorgio Pasqualin

Rising From Unsustainable: Replacing Automobiles and Rockets—J.P. Sweeney

Food—Life's Gift for Healing: Simple, Delicious & Life Saving Whole Food Plant Based Solutions—Angel and Terry Grier

Harmonize All of You With All: The Leap Ahead in Self-Development—Artie Vipperla

Powerless to Powerful: How to Stop Living in Fear and Start Living Your Life—Kat Spencer

Living with Dirty Glasses: How to Clean those Dirty Glasses and Gain a Clearer Perspective Of Your Life—Leah Montani

The Road Back to You: Finding Your Way After Losing a Child to Suicide—Trish Simonson

Gavin Gone: Turning Pain into Purpose to Create a Legacy—Rita Gladding

The Health Nexus: TMJ, Sleep Apnea, and Facial Development, Causations and Treatment—Robert Perkins DDS

Samantha Jean's Rainbow Dream: A Young Foster Girl's Adventure into the Colorful World of Fruits & Vegetables—AJ Autieri-Luciano

Live Your Truth: An Arab Man's Journey In Finding the Courage to Live His Truth As He Identifies as Gay and Coping with Mental Illness—David Rabadi

Unstoppable: A Parent's Survival Guide for Special Education Services with an IEP or 504 Plan—Raja B. Marhaba

Please, Excuse My Brave: Overcoming Fear and Living Out Your Purpose—Anisa Wesley

Drawing with Purpose: A Sketch Journal—Rick Alonzo

NY Coffee: Love Fulfilled in the Little Things—Craig Lieckfelt

Good Work: How Gen X and Millennials are the Dream Team for Doing Good When Collaborating—Erin Kate Whitcomb

Rescue Me: Guided Self-Healing for First Responders: Conquering Depression, Anxiety, PTSD & Moral Injury—David Hogan

Treasures In Grief: Discover 7 Spiritual Gifts Hidden in Your Pain—Lo Anne Mayer

We Three: Their Beginnings—Derek Drummond

Ripping off the Mask—Joseph Lee

Culture Spin—Kristy Wachter

Discover Your Inner Leader—Mamta Goyal

Grit, Growth and Gumption for Women: Three Keys To Lead Yourself and Others With Confidence—Tinsley English

www.ingramcontent.com/pod-product-compliance
Lightning Source LLC
Chambersburg PA
CBHW022001150726
47990CB00002B/548